NEW ORLEANS
COCKTAILS

AN ELEGANT COLLECTION
OF OVER 100 RECIPES
INSPIRED BY THE BIG EASY

SARAH BAIRD

CIDER MILL
PRESS

BOOK
PUBLISHERS
KENNEBUNKPORT, MAINE

13-Digit ISBN: 978-1604336436

10-Digit ISBN: 1604336439

This book may be ordered by mail from the publisher. Please include $5.99 for postage and handling. Please support your local bookseller first!

Books published by Cider Mill Press Book Publishers are available at special discounts for bulk purchases in the United States by corporations, institutions, and other organizations. For more information, please contact the publisher.

Cider Mill Press Book Publishers

"Where good books are ready for press"

PO Box 454

12 Spring Street

Kennebunkport, Maine 04046

Visit us online! www.cidermillpress.com

Typography: Copperplate, Mercury, Rennie Mackintosh, Ribbon

Image Credits: Photos on pages 38, 39, 52, 54–55, 67, 85, 94, 138–139, 148–149, 178, 200–201, 218–219, 224–225, 229, 233, 234–235, 278, 279 copyright Cheryl Gerber, used with permission; Pages 25 and 27 courtesy of The Roosevelt New Orleans, a Waldorf Astoria Hotel; Pages 9, 12, 15, 20, 21, 30, 32, 33, and 186 courtesy of Arnaud's; Page 46 courtesy of Tujague's; Pages 69 and 208 courtesy of SouBou; Pages 88 and 216 courtesy of Sharon Pye; Page 92 courtesy of Sara Essex Bradley; Pages 106, 171, and 252 courtesy of Juliana Argentino; Page 118 courtesy of Todd Coleman; Page 121 courtesy of Antoine's; Pages 162–163 Library of Congress; Page 185 courtesy of Melanie Kunz Estopinal; Page 212 courtesy of Josh Brasted; page 243 courtesy of Vince Murray; pages 244 and 245 Library of Congress; Page 251 courtesy of T. Cole Newton

Printed in China

6 7 8 9 0

CONTENTS

 INTRODUCTION

New Orleans is a city that inspires a great deal of romantic loyalty, even from those who don't live there.

Just casually mention that you're from New Orleans in any public setting—airport, baby shower, in line at the DMV—and watch everyone's eyes immediately sparkle.

"We come every year during Mardi Gras! Once Harry Connick, Jr., pointed at me from a float during Orpheus," a woman will swoon, her heart clearly still beating fast over the encounter.

"I grew up idolizing Professor Longhair," a man will say in awe. "When I was 21, I got to see him play the Maple Leaf. I still have the coaster from that night."

Like a live-action fever dream, New Orleans is a place that reminds people life is meant to be lived in the now, and that spontaneity—an impromptu porch-sitting session with neighbors, hearing a brass band giving a spur-of-the-moment street corner performance—beats structure any day of the week.

Cocktails lie at the very heart of this culture, and today (dare I say it?) are more important than ever. High-end bartenders are not only steeped in New Orleans classics top-to-bottom—pretty much everyone can make a mighty fine Sazerac—but over the past ten years, the city has built one of the country's strongest, most forward-thinking drinking communities. There's a degree of reverence for New Orleans' rich tippling tradition in every glass, and bartenders are constantly finding ways to honor the past while keeping an eye toward the future.

New Orleans has also long served as a temporary home for artists and makers magnetized and electrified by the city's swirl of performance art. It's a place where people feel free to let their freak flag fly without thinking twice. Want to roll down the street in a rabbit mask and hot-pink ball gown? New Orleans says, *go for it!* This also means, thanks to programs like Tales of the Cocktail (see page 181), that the city has started to draw some of the country's top bartending talent who have fallen under its spell while visiting and decided, "Oh, maybe I'll just stick around." Cocktail-making is, after all, a very special kind of live-action show.

If you're looking to capture a small piece of New Orleans but can't charter a flight for a Ramos Gin Fizz, this book will allow you to stir, shake, sip, and imagine that you're on a sweet olive-covered balcony in the Crescent City.

A MAGNIFICENTLY BRIEF HISTORY OF NEW ORLEANS COCKTAILS

For most people, it's hard to think about New Orleans without liquor springing to mind.

While other cities spread out their affection between beer, wine, and cocktails, New Orleans has always been more of a singular spirits-driven affair. Whether your imbibing memories take you to julep-fueled, live-oak-shaded garden soirées or to bachelorette parties full of Bourbon Street concoctions, it's a city undoubtedly built on a boozy foundation.

It's also a place of larger-than-life drinking lore. New Orleanians are natural-born storytellers and we love to talk about our beloved city almost more than anything. This is particularly true when it comes to our holy trinity: booze, food, and music. You'd be hard pressed to find a resident who doesn't have a favorite spot to snag red beans and rice on a Monday night, listen to jazz, or while away the afternoon with a frozen daiquiri. In turn, it's almost impossible to separate out the three from one another, forever knotted up in a bundle of joyful decadence.

Sometimes amidst so much revelry, though, fact and fiction can get a little garbled. For generations, New Orleanians have passed down the story that the cocktail was actually invented in our fair city by the pharmacist Antoine Peychaud—who would add his signature bitters to nips of brandy in coquetiers (egg cups in French). As the story goes, coquetier was corrupted into the word "cocktail," and, lo, the term was born.

The truth, however, happens to be a little bit different. In the mid-2000s, dutiful researchers from the Museum of the American Cocktail (yes, we have a cocktail museum here) discovered references to "cocktails" dating back as early as 1806.

So, did we invent the cocktail? Well, no.

Did we gussy it up, breathe new life into it, and give it over 175 years (and counting) of inventive iterations?

Absolutely.

Starting with the Sazerac in the mid-1800s, we've added—and continue to add—cocktail after cocktail to the international cannon of classics, including (but not limited to) the Brandy Crusta, Grasshopper, Ramos Gin Fizz, Hurricane, and Brandy Milk Punch. We took a page from France's playbook and showed the United States how to do absinthe right, with frappes and drips. The city also remains the foremost place in the country devoted to a strange, antiquated Spanish liqueur known as Ojen. And with all this, we've barely touched the lip of the glass when it comes to what New Orleans has contributed to the global drinking scene. (Don't worry, you'll learn all about that and more in the pages ahead.)

We also count among our ranks innumerable famous (although temporary) residents heavily influenced by our seemingly limitless libations. From Tennessee Williams and Truman Capote to Charles Bukowski and Walker Percy, the affection of these literary giants for New Orleans' drinking culture is impossible to miss in their prose.

In the twentieth century, New Orleans also quietly, steadily, altered the course of national cocktail history. The parents of Donn the Beachcomber—the founder of tiki—operated a hotel here, and the city's laidback, freewheeling ways undoubtedly found their way into the Donn's DNA. One of the most important post-Prohibition cocktail books, *Famous New Orleans Drinks and How to Mix 'Em* (1937), focuses squarely on the innate importance of cocktail culture in the City that Care Forgot.

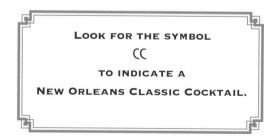

LOOK FOR THE SYMBOL

CC

TO INDICATE A

NEW ORLEANS CLASSIC COCKTAIL.

And now, with the New Orleans-based Tales of the Cocktail event well into its teenage years and more enthusiasm swirling than ever before about the revival of high-end drinking culture, we sit at a sterling moment in the history of New Orleans drinking.

Truly, there's been no better time to raise a glass to the Crescent City.

TECHNIQUES AND PREPARATIONS

Many of the cocktails in this book use some of the same techniques and preparations, so I've compiled them here in an effort to not be repetitive. Whenever a common technique or preparation is listed in a recipe, you can refer back here to see how it's done. These are listed in alphabetical order.

ABSINTHE MIST: Fill a small, travel-sized spray bottle with absinthe. Coat the inside of the glass with 1–2 sprays.

DRY SHAKE: In a cocktail tin, combine ingredients without ice and shake. This technique is usually used in drinks involving egg white, in order to emulsify it.

DOUBLE STRAIN: Single straining is done using the traditional Hawthorne strainer and will be what's required for most drinks. Some cocktails, though, require two filters to create a more velvety mouthfeel. To double strain, place a fine mesh strainer over the glass and pour your drink, first through the Hawthorne strainer and then through the mesh. Voila!

RICH SIMPLE SYRUP (2:1): In a small saucepan, combine 2 cups granulated sugar with 1 cup water. Stir over medium heat, until sugar is completely dissolved. Let cool to room temperature, then store in an airtight container, refrigerated, for up to 1 week. For demerara syrup, replace granulated sugar with demerara sugar.

SHORT SHAKE: A short shake is a little less vigorous and time consuming than a traditional shake. Essentially, you just want to mix all the ingredients and chill the drink.

SIMPLE SYRUP (1:1): In a small saucepan, combine 1 cup granulated sugar and 1 cup water. Stir over medium heat, until sugar is completely dissolved. Let cool to room temperature, then store in an airtight container, refrigerated, for up to 1 week. For demerara syrup, replace granulated sugar with demerara sugar.

SUGARED RIM: Fill one small bowl with ¼ cup water and one with ¼ granulated sugar. Dip the mouth of a glass first in the bowl filled with water, and then in the bowl filled with sugar.

WHIP SHAKE: A whip shake means to really give your biceps a workout and shake that bad boy as hard as you can (preferably with two hands) with a very—*very*—small amount of ice (say, one cube). For example, in the Ramos Gin Fizz, it's important to create the creamy consistency found within the drink.

FIRST TIME TIPS
FOR DRINKING IN NEW ORLEANS

Being in New Orleans to imbibe for the first time can seem a little, well, overwhelming, even for a seasoned cocktail enthusiast. Below are a few basic rules to make sure you're pulling it off like a pro.

1. The Ramos Gin Fizz is a brunch drink.
Ordering a Ramos Gin Fizz after brunch hours is kind of like asking for Eggs Benedict at 8 p.m.: You're not going to make any friends that way. Instead, ask for literally any other cocktail on the planet until the sun starts to rise, then a Ramos is fair game again. Also, be a friend and don't order one if the bar is slammed—your bartender will thank you.

2. Take your drinking tour outside the French Quarter.
Sure, the French Quarter is the neon-drenched, pastel-hued heartbeat of the city, but there's so much more to New Orleans' eclectic cocktail culture. Rent a bike, slap on some rollerskates, hop in a cab—just promise me you'll venture outside your comfort zone.

3. See live music with a drink in hand.
Whether jazz, swing, death metal (or all of the above) is your thing, there's a completely liquor-drenched music venue with your name on it. A trip to New Orleans isn't complete without losing track of time while sipping a drink, totally immersed in your New Favorite Band.

4. Hydration is no joke.
New Orleans' subtropical temperatures are enough to make a person practically wilt—and that's without any drinks in them. The "one water for every cocktail" rule is not just a gentle suggestion here: it should probably be some sort of law.

5. If you're going to drink a beer, make sure to sip local.
New Orleans has become a hotbed for local breweries in recent years, and there's no excuse not to try the local suds when you're in town. Whether you're reaching for a classic, like the Abita Amber, or something from a smaller micro-distillery like the recently opened Urban South, try to keep it within state lines.

6. Take a stroll down Bourbon Street—if only once.
It goes without saying not to overindulge on Bourbon Street, but there is something that can be delightfully otherworldly about the entire experience. Take a night to get it out of your system—parade around with a Technicolor Hand Grenade in your clutches, request a song at Pat O'Brien's piano—then head off to other spots.

7. Take advantage of go cups.
When you arrive in New Orleans, you'll quickly learn that asking for a go cup (aka, a to-go cup) is a super-slick move. You can drink on the streets, after all, so why not take advantage of it as much as possible? It would be downright rude to let a good drink go half finished.

Oh, and if anyone asks you where you got your shoes? The answer is, "On my feet."

APÉRITIF/DIJESTIF: A drink that stimulates your appetite or a drink that helps you digest your meal. Examples of apéritifs are Suze and soda, any champagne-based cocktail, Lillet, or a kir. Dijestifs are drinks made with brandy, Chartreuse, Bénédictine, or calvados.

BITTERS: There are two different categories of bitters. There bitter-flavored liqueurs, which are used as additions or as the base for a variety of cocktails. Examples include Campari, Suze, Aperol, Amaro, and Cocchi Rosa. There are also bitters that are infused, very flavorful alcohol-based liquids used in extremely small quantities to flavor a cocktail. They come in small bottles, with the most well-known being Angostura bitters. They are made by a variety of companies and come in a myriad of flavors such as orange, chocolate, celery, and lavender, to name but a few.

> **A NOTE ON BITTERS:** *Bitters are a key ingredient in today's craft cocktails. Stock up on a variety of flavors. There are a number of excellent companies making bitters in the U.S. and beyond including Bitter End, Fee's, Scrappy's, Bob's, and Bittermans. Celery is one of the most common flavor profiles. A sampler pack, which several of the companies offer, is a great idea.*

CORDIALS: A sweet substance made from fruit or flowers that is added to a cocktail or drunk alone. In the United States, cordials are thought of as alcoholic and in the UK and elsewhere they are typically non-alcoholic.

LIQUEUR: An alcoholic substance that is typically sweeter than a liquor and made by combining a distilled spirit with something sweet and flavorful such as fruit, coffee, cream, chocolate, herbs, or spices. Examples are cassis, Kahlúa, Irish cream, crème de menthe, and Grand Marnier.

VERMOUTH: Dry vermouth is white; sweet vermouth is red. France is more famous for its dry and Italy for its sweet. As in most things, the brand and quality matter.

LIQUOR: Alcoholic substance made from grains, plants, or sugar cane and fermented to be drunk straight or combined and used as the base of a cocktail. Examples are rum, vodka, gin, brandy, tequila, whiskey, and cachaça (a sugar cane–based alcohol made in Brazil).

SYRUPS: There is simple syrup, which is sugar heated in water so that it dissolves, and flavored syrups, which are made in the same fashion but have added a flavor profile such as ginger, lemongrass, lime, or passion fruit. These are used to sweeten and add flavor to a cocktail. Some syrups can be bought ready-made; an example is Grenadine which is actually a pomegranate syrup.

FRENCH QUARTER
CLASSIC COCKTAILS

Without a doubt, the French Quarter is the heartbeat of imbibing culture in the city. From the neon glitz of Bourbon Street to the refined, wood-paneled bars of the neighborhood's stately hotels, there's a little bit of something for every kind of imbiber and—more than any other place in the United States—cocktail lovers flock here in droves.

"NEW ORLEANS IS A PLACE WHERE WE DON'T TRY TO HIDE OUR DRINKING. THANKS TO GO CUPS AND LAX LIQUOR LAWS, WE DO IT ON OUR FRONT PORCHES AND IN THE STREETS. IT'S A WAY OF LIFE, AND COCKTAILS IN THE FRENCH QUARTER ARE AT THE CENTER OF IT ALL."

—Elizabeth Pearce, a drinks historian who operates the French Quarter Drinking Tour

❧ SAZERAC ❧

You can't go two feet in New Orleans without a bartender telling you the in-depth history of the city's golden cocktail, the Sazerac. Believed (erroneously) by many New Orleanians to have been the first-ever cocktail, the Sazerac might not have pioneered the mixed drink—I mean, come on, folks figured that out long ago—but it certainly raised the bar.

GLASSWARE: Old Fashioned glass
GARNISH: Lemon peel

- **2 sugar cubes**
- **1¼ oz Herbsaint, divided**
- **5–7 dashes Peychaud's bitters**
- **2 oz rye whiskey**

TO ASSEMBLE:

1. Fill an Old Fashioned glass with ice and set aside.

2. In a mixing glass, add two sugar cubes followed by ¾ ounces of the Herbsaint, and the bitters.

3. Muddle, add the rye, and continue to muddle.

4. Add ice and stir until diluted and chilled.

5. Empty the ice-filled Old Fashioned glass. Coat the glass with the remaining ½-ounce of the Herbsaint and spin. Give a quick dump, leaving a small puddle of Herbsaint in the bottom.

6. Strain the cocktail from the mixing glass into the Herbsaint-rinsed Old Fashioned glass.

7. Garnish with lemon peel.

Around 1850, New Orleanian Sewell T. Taylor began importing a cognac brand by the name of Sazerac de Forge et Fils, inspiring budding entrepreneur Aaron Bird to rebrand his newly acquired bar, conveniently, Sazerac House. Its main specialty was the Sazerac Cocktail, made with a little from column A—cognac—and a little from column B—bitters made by druggist Antoine Peychaud. It was an instant hit. By hook or by crook, rye eventually replaced cognac as the spirit of choice, but little else has changed about the drink since its birth. It's still the spirit-forward, slow sipper it was during the days of ladies flashing ankle instead of, well, other things. The version on the previous page, crafted by Arnaud's French 75's Chris Hannah, is about as classically perfect as you can get, though many industry insiders believe that Empire Bar's Paul Gustings serves the city's best version of the drink.

BAR SPOTLIGHT

SAZERAC BAR
The Roosevelt New Orleans
130 Roosevelt Way
New Orleans, LA 70112
Phone: (504) 648-1200
www.therooseveltneworleans.com

Recently reopened inside the Roosevelt Hotel, the Sazerac Bar is a destination location for cocktail enthusiasts looking to sip the city's signature libation. An Art Deco landmark through and through, after you've had your fill of Sazeracs, try something on the lighter side like the Thibodaux Tickle: gin, rhubarb bitters, cranberry bitters, sugar, and soda.

FUN FACT: THE SAZERAC WAS NAMED THE OFFICIAL LOUISIANA STATE COCKTAIL IN 2008.

TAYLOR BIRD SAZERAC

When you have a drink as ubiquitous as the Sazerac, it's bound to inspire some clever plays. The two takes here pull from different aspects of New Orleans heritage: Cajun and Caribbean. The star of this Sazerac variation is Steen's cane syrup, a sticky-sweet Louisiana favorite from Acadiana with a flavor somewhere between maple syrup and sorghum. It is, without a doubt, worth seeking out. *Attributed to Abigail Gullo at Compére Lapin.*

GLASSWARE: Sazerac glass

GARNISH: Lemon twist

- 1 oz cognac
- 1 oz rye whiskey
- ¼ oz Steen's cane syrup
- 2 dashes orange bitters
- 6 dashes Peychaud's bitters
- Absinthe, for misting

TO ASSEMBLE:

1. In a mixing glass half-full of ice, combine all ingredients except absinthe. Stir.

2. Pour into a chilled Sazerac glass that has been misted with absinthe (see page 13).

3. Serve up, garnished with lemon twist.

CUBAN SAZERAC

The Sazerac goes to the islands with this banana-tinged, rum-based creation.

Attributed to Alan Walters at Loa.

GLASSWARE: Rocks glass

GARNISH: Lemon twist

- ⅛ oz Herbsaint
- 2 oz rum, preferably Matusalem Gran Reserva 18 Year
- ¼ oz banana syrup
- 2 dashes Peychaud's bitters

To Assemble:

1. Coat the inside of a rocks glass with Herbsaint, spin, and discard excess.

2. In a mixing glass with ice, combine rum, syrup, and bitters. Stir.

3. Strain into Herbsaint-coated rocks glass.

4. Garnish with lemon twist.

BAR SPOTLIGHT

FRENCH 75

813 Bienville St
New Orleans, LA 70112
Phone: (504) 523-5433
www.arnaudsrestaurant.com

A dimly-lit, diminutive bar tucked off of famed restaurant Arnaud's, James Beard finalist French 75 has become a darling of the New Orleans food and drink literati over the past decade, thanks in large part to the cult following around beloved bartender Chris Hannah, whose commitment to revitalizing classic cocktails helped to usher in their revival both locally and nationally. Outside of Hannah—who sports a signature white jacket—the bar staff all don tuxes as they deliver drinks to guests lounging on leopard print couches, giving a sophisticated, cigar-bar-style air to the space.

⤳ FRENCH 75, ARNAUD'S STYLE ⤳

The French 75—widely known for having gin as its primary liquor-of-choice—was, in truth, originally made with cognac. The traditional styling was brought back into the spotlight by Chris Hannah, and has launched a wave of debate over cognac vs. gin as the ideal spirit within the bubbly, tart drink. If you're going the New Orleans way, drink it like it's done on Bienville Street. *Attributed to Chris Hannah at French 75.*

GLASSWARE: Champagne flute

GARNISH: Lemon twist

- **1¼ oz cognac, preferably Courvoisier VS**
- **¼ oz fresh lemon juice**
- **¼ oz simple syrup (see page 14)**
- **Champagne (chilled), to top, preferably Chandon Imperial**

TO ASSEMBLE:

1. In a cocktail tin filled with ice, combine cognac, lemon juice, and simple syrup. Shake.

2. Strain into champagne flute and top with champagne.

3. Garnish with a lemon twist.

HAVING A DRINK WITH...

CHRIS HANNAH OF FRENCH 75

Chris Hannah, the head bartender at Arnaud's French 75, is one of the best known characters in the New Orleans (and global) cocktail scene. His decade-plus commitment to not only lovingly crafting cocktails five nights a week for his guests, but spreading the gospel of New Orleans cocktails across the globe, has made him something of a living legend. Below, Hannah talks about jazz music, Casablanca, *and how New Orleans was his escape from "Everyday USA."*

SB: When you were a kid, what did you want to be?

CH: I guess I wanted to work around parties, like in cool old movies where all the fancy people are getting champagne from trays. I wanted to do that. I just kind of figured the only way to be at the party was if I worked it. It's not that Humphrey Bogart isn't cool [in *Casablanca*], but I didn't think I would be Humphrey Bogart, I thought I would be like on a team, you know, making the drinks, stuff like that. It would be good if I were the piano player.

SB: Well, piano dreams aside, you definitely have achieved that goal. What brought you to New Orleans?

CH: I always wanted to live in New Orleans. I have an old soul. I moved here for the jazz...and to be able to dress like Louis Armstrong.

SB: But seriously.

CH: New Orleans kind of let me open my eyes. It's like, I knew there were some jazz songs, but until you get down here you don't realize that there are that many. I knew about Louis Armstrong before I moved here, but I never knew about Danny Barker. I don't see why everything has to be normal, and that's the reason why I moved here, because I didn't want to be. I was trying to escape "Everyday USA."

SB: What drew you to French 75?

CH: I knew that it should be something. It's a beautiful room, the restaurant's really nice. When I walked in that bar, it just looked absolutely beautiful, and I felt like I didn't want it to rest on its laurels like a lot of bars in New Orleans were doing. I knew that new drinks were going to be big again. I didn't know that it was going to be as big as they are, but I had a lot of friends in New York and San Francisco already, and I kind of wanted to do the same thing that they were doing. I just wanted to prove that something old could actually be at the same level as like, PDT, but not be a new bar.

SB: Everyone in bartending seems to move around a lot. Why have you stayed at French 75?

CH: Some people think it's unique to have somebody at a bar for that long, and I'm starting to understand that. One minute you move down and, the next thing you know, you're there at the same bar for twelve years. I feel like we're on a mission every time we're there to have all the guests happy: happy they came in, and happy to come back.

FUN FACT: A LONGSTANDING TRADITION AT FRENCH 75 IS TO WRITE RECOMMENDATIONS FOR GUESTS ON THE BACK OF BAR NAPKINS. BARTENDER HADI KTIRI HAS TAKEN THIS PRACTICE TO THE INTERNET, WHERE HE RUNS NAPKIN LOCAL.

⌇ BRANDY CRUSTA ⌇

Abeautifully prepared drink that paved the way for the likes of the Sidecar, the Brandy Crusta was reportedly invented in 1852 by Joseph Santina at a bar called the Jewel of the South on Gravier Street. It's the drink's delicately sugared rim and long, twirling lemon peel that delights the eye, but make no mistake about it, this is no session drink: it packs a wallop of citrus-tinged booze.

GLASSWARE: Cocktail glass
GARNISH: Sugared rim, lemon peel

- **1¾ oz cognac**
- **¾ oz lemon juice**
- **½ oz orange curaçao**
- **¼ oz maraschino liqueur**
- **2 dashes Angostura bitters**

TO ASSEMBLE:

1. In a cocktail tin with ice, combine all ingredients. Shake.

2. Strain into a chilled and sugar-rimmed cocktail glass (see page 14).

3. Garnish with peel of entire lemon.

⌒ ARNAUD'S SPECIAL COCKTAIL ⌒

Popularized at its namesake restaurant during the 1940s and a kissing cousin to the Rob Roy, the Arnaud's Special Cocktail allows the smoky notes of Scotch to shine through while tempering its often finicky (and polarizing) bite with the sweetness of Dubonnet—an aromatic, wine-based aperitif—and citrus notes.

GLASSWARE: Rocks glass

GARNISH: Orange twist

- **2 oz Scotch**
- **1 oz Dubonnet**
- **3 dashes orange bitters**

TO ASSEMBLE:

1. In a cocktail tin, combine all ingredients. Shake.

2. Strain into rocks glass.

3. Garnish with an orange twist.

FUN FACT: DUBONNET WAS ORIGINALLY CREATED IN 1847 TO HELP FRENCH SOLDIERS TAKE THE EDGE OFF BEING TREATED WITH QUININE.

CAROUSEL BAR

Hotel Monteleone
214 Royal St
New Orleans, LA 70130
Phone: (504) 523-3341
www.hotelmonteleone.com/entertainment/carousel-bar

First things first about the much ballyhooed Carousel Bar inside the Hotel Monteleone: Yes, it really does spin around. While sitting on a whimsical stool carved into the shape of a lion or giraffe, the bar's slow revolution is charming, spirited, and—after a few drinks—can be a little trippy. More than almost any other spot, it speaks to how fine cocktail craftsmanship and a healthy dose of playfulness are hallmarks of the New Orleans drinking experience.

VIEUX CARRE

For what it's worth, I believe the Vieux Carre to be the sexiest of all the drinks in the classic New Orleans cannon. Strong, stirred, and named after the Francophone term for the French Quarter, it's the kind of drink that seems ripe for a night of getting into trouble in alleyways around town. Invented in the 1930s by Walter Bergeron at the Monteleone, its sultry finish and mysterious air feels kind of like sipping a little piece of New Orleans in a glass.

GLASSWARE: Old Fashioned glass
GARNISH: Lemon twist

- ½ oz **Bénédictine liqueur**
- ½ oz **rye whiskey**
- ½ oz **cognac**
- ½ oz **sweet vermouth**
- 1 dash **Peychaud's bitters**
- 1 dash **Angostura bitters**

TO ASSEMBLE:

1. In a chilled Old Fashioned glass with ice, combine all ingredients. Stir.

2. Garnish with lemon twist.

⤳ PIMM'S CUP ⤳

Sure, the Pimm's Cup is far and away one of the most British drinks imaginable, sipped for decades on the sidelines at Wimbledon and after foxhunts through the moors. But it's also been a staple at the 200-plus-year-old Chartres Street watering hole Napoleon House since the 1940s. While Napoleon himself never waltzed through the doors, the space was offered up to the Frenchman in 1821 as a place of refuge during his exile. The name stuck, and little seems to have changed since then: the bar's romantically crumbling walls are lined top-to-bottom with framed clippings and oil paintings that speak to its storied past.

GLASSWARE: Collins glass

GARNISH: Cucumber sliver

- **1¼ oz Pimm's #1**
- **3 oz lemonade**
- **7-Up, to top**

TO ASSEMBLE:

1. In a Collins glass half-filled with ice, combine Pimm's and lemonade. Stir.

2. Top with 7-Up, and garnish with cucumber sliver.

BAR SPOTLIGHT

ACE HOTEL

600 Carondelet St
New Orleans, LA 70130
Phone: (504) 900-1180
www.acehotel.com/neworleans

The first Ace outpost in the South chose to be anchored in New Orleans, and with good reason: What other city has a commitment as deep and abiding to supporting artists that are

risk-taking and—occasionally—bizarre? Every drink-focused area of the hotel is a stunner, from the restaurant bar at Josephine Estelle to the velvet-draped lobby bar to Alto, a rooftop bar and restaurant accented with all the tropical charm imaginable.

EMPIRE BAR AT BROUSSARD'S

819 Conti St
New Orleans, LA 70112
Phone: (504) 581-3866
www.broussards.com/news/
empire-bar/647

Helmed by the New Orleans' bartending community's most charming curmudgeon, Paul Gustings, the lavishly renovated Empire Bar at Broussard's is the kind of place to visit when you're looking to impress a date (while sipping some

Empire Bar

of the city's finest libations). The bar also opens out onto a luxurious courtyard, which is ripe for happy hour drinking after spring showers. Anything created by Mr. Gustings is sure to be a gem, but make sure not to miss the Leite de Onça—cachaça, toasted coconut shavings, pineapple syrup, heavy cream, condensed milk, and Mexican chocolate—a drink that's as rich as it is tropical.

TUJAGUE'S

823 Decatur St
New Orleans, LA 70116
Phone: (504) 525-8676
www.tujaguesrestaurant.com

Tujague's

Established in 1856 and moved to its present location in 1914, Tujague's holds the honor of being New Orleans' second-oldest drinking establishment and the first "standing bar" in the city. The long-stretching bar was crafted sans barstools so day laborers could pound a quick drink and head back out to work—no need for all that fancy sitting business. Today, the bar feels nothing if not deeply historic, decked out in dark wood and with a famed back bar imported from France in the nineteenth century.

∽ RAMOS GIN FIZZ ∽

Frothy, heady, and the ultimate tall, creamy, handsome sipper, the Ramos Gin Fizz is the quintessential New Orleans brunch drink.

GLASSWARE: Collins glass

GARNISH: None

- **2 oz gin**
- **1 oz half-and-half**
- **¾ oz simple syrup (see page 14)**
- **½ oz lemon juice**
- **½ oz lime juice**
- **2 dashes orange blossom water**
- **1 egg white**
- **Soda, to top**

TO ASSEMBLE:

1. In a cocktail tin, combine all ingredients. Dry shake (see page 13) for 15–20 seconds.

2. Fill cocktail tin one-quarter full with ice and whip shake (see page 14) for 3–5 minutes.

3. Pour into a chilled Collins glass and top with soda until foamy head forms.

Invented in 1888 by Henry C. Ramos at the long-gone Imperial Cabinet Saloon (R.I.P.), the **RAMOS GIN FIZZ** was originally known as the New Orleans Fizz, but renamed in honor of Ramos years later at the Sazerac Bar. A favorite of Huey P. Long, the larger-than-life Louisiana governor and bon vivant once flew a New Orleans bartender to New York to show bartenders up north how to properly craft the creation so it was never too far out of his reach. For those itching to take a field trip, Ramos is buried in Jefferson Parish, about a fifteen-minute drive from the French Quarter. Each year during Tales of the Cocktail, a group of bartenders make a pilgrimage to pay their respects. Some advice: Unless you want to immediately get on a bartender's bad side, don't order one of these labor-intensive creations—which take minutes on end to shake properly—when the bar is slammed with guests.

⤳ GRASSHOPPER ⤳

This minty, creamy after-dinner cocktail was created, according to legend, sometime in the 1920s by Philip Guichet of Tujague's. It took second prize in a 1928 New York drink competition, and has been a dessert-like favorite of drinkers with a sweet tooth ever since.

❧

GLASSWARE: Cocktail glass

GARNISH: None

- **1 oz green crème de menthe**
- **1 oz white crème de cacao**
- **1 oz cream**

TO ASSEMBLE:

1. In a cocktail tin filled with ice, combine all ingredients. Shake.

2. Strain into a chilled cocktail glass.

ABSINTHE

No city in the United States has a level of zealot-like passion for "the green fairy" (a.k.a. absinthe) quite like New Orleans, where the licorice-flavored, herbal liqueur has been enjoyed by imbibers strutting up and down Royal Street since it found its way from France in the mid-1830s.

Made from a distilled menagerie of herbs including anise, wormwood, lemon balm, fennel, and licorice, the glistening drink gained notoriety in the city during the late 1800s for being particularly potent, causing drinkers to get ahead of themselves very quickly. While absinthe's high proof—which typically hovers around 60 percent—is the likely culprit for folks getting a little too giddy, the herb wormwood (used for medicinal purposes across Europe for centuries) was blamed. Drinkers began reporting muscle spasms and hallucinations after downing one too many absinthe-based concoctions, and the drink was banned in 1912.

It wasn't until 2007 that the spirit was once again allowed to be served (legally) at bars in the United States , and thankfully, there's nothing standing between you and a classically-prepared absinthe drip these days.

ABSINTHE SUSSINSSE

An orange-tinged brunch cocktail with a hint of mint, the Absinthe Sussinsse gained popularity in the early part of the twentieth century as an early-morning pick-me-up. After absinthe was banned in 1912, it largely fell off the drinking radar, but is ripe for a comeback in the wake of the spirit's stateside rebirth.

GLASSWARE: Wine glass

GARNISH: None

- **1 oz absinthe**
- **½ oz Herbsaint**
- **½ oz créme de menthe**
- **1 oz heavy cream**
- **¼ oz simple syrup (see page 14)**
- **1 dash orange flower water**
- **1 egg white**

TO ASSEMBLE:

1. In a cocktail tin, combine all ingredients. Dry shake (see page 19) 10–15 seconds.

2. Add ice and shake until combined.

3. Strain into a chilled wine glass.

⌒ ABSINTHE FRAPPE ⌒

Created by bartender Cayetano Ferrer at the Old Absinthe House in 1874, it's imperative to sip one at the place of its creation during any trip to the city.

GLASSWARE: Julep cup

GARNISH: Mint sprig

- 1½ oz absinthe
- ¼ oz simple syrup (see page 14)
- 2 oz soda water
- 1 dash anisette

To Assemble:

1. In a cocktail tin half-filled with ice, combine all ingredients. Shake.

2. Strain into a julep cup filled with crushed ice.

3. Top with a mound of additional ice.

~ ABSINTHE DRIP ~

At swanky establishments, this dribbled cocktail is served from an elegant tool called an absinthe fountain, through an absinthe spoon, and into an absinthe glass. At home, a slotted spoon balanced over the lip of an Old Fashioned glass will do the trick.

GLASSWARE: Old Fashioned cup
GARNISH: None

- **1 oz absinthe**
- **1 sugar cube**
- **4–5 oz ice water**

TO ASSEMBLE:

1. In an Old Fashioned glass, pour absinthe.

2. Place a slotted or absinthe spoon on top of the glass, and place the sugar cube on top of the spoon.

3. Very slowly, begin to drip ice water over the cube and into the glass until the sugar cube is mostly dissolved and the absinthe begins to look opalescent and cloudy.

4. Stir any remaining sugar into the cocktail until dissolved.

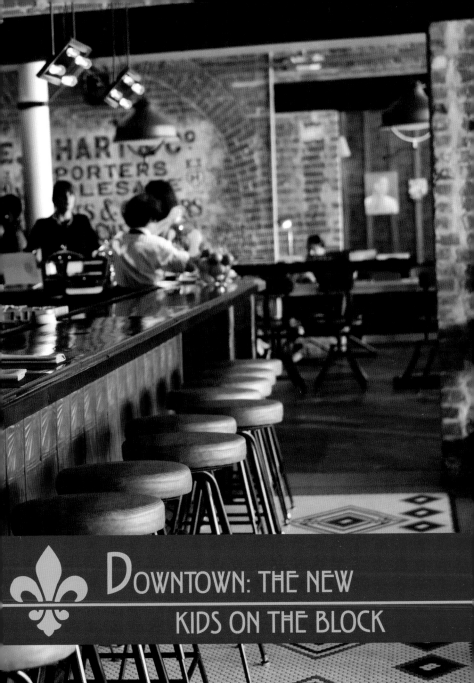

DOWNTOWN: THE NEW
KIDS ON THE BLOCK

The French Quarter has an unparalleled pedigree when it comes to watering holes, its winding alleyways and cobbled nooks bursting forth with secret dives and under-the-radar places to snag a quick drink (and air-conditioning) on a muggy summer afternoon.

Today, this rich legacy is expanding not only within the Vieux Carré, but into parts of downtown once primarily reserved strictly for office workers grabbing business lunches (and, probably, a few stealthy drinks). Below are some of the strongest up-and-comers within the pastel-hued French Quarter as well as the neighboring Central Business and Warehouse Districts.

"THE INHABITANTS [OF NEW ORLEANS]...
ARE UNIVERSALLY CONSIDERED AS THE
MOST REFINED AND ARISTOCRATIC
MEMBERS OF SOCIETY ON THE
CONTINENT."

—*Alexander St. Clair-Abrams*
in The Trials of the Soldier's Wife, 1864

BAR SPOTLIGHT

BALISE

640 Carondelet St
New Orleans, LA 70130
Phone: (504) 459-4449
www.balisenola.com

With a knack for taking difficult-to-use ingredients and show-casing how they can become the star of the show (with a little bit of tweaking), Balise bar manager Jesse Carr has built a cocktail program that is as deep and—occasionally—mysterious as the nearby Mississippi River. Named after a Louisiana ghost town, the leath-er and wood nautically-themed restaurant is the Central Busi-ness District sibling to Justin Devillier's much-celebrated Uptown spot La Petite Grocery.

ANGELINE

1032 Chartres St
New Orleans, LA 70116
Phone: (504) 308-3106
www.angelinenola.com

With a focus on finely-tuned Southern cuisine with smart-ly placed touches from the Mediterranean, this relative newcomer from Chef Alex Har-rell has already gained a loyal following. The bar program boasts one of the city's stron-gest and smartest selections of smoky mezcal, and has also

Angeline

become a go-to destination for sherry lovers to indulge.

KINGFISH

337 Chartres St
New Orleans, LA 70130
Phone: (504) 598-5005
www.kingfishneworleans.com

Kingfish might not be an old timer in the French Quarter, but its cocktail pedigree got off on the right foot. The drinks program at this tradition-adoring joint was originally helmed by the godfather of New Orleans cocktails, Chris McMillan, who has since gone on to open his own bar and restaurant, Revel, in Mid-City. McMillan's attentiveness is still felt in each drink, from his interpretation of Creole Coffee to the Cable Car. (Part-time residents Beyoncé and Jay-Z visit frequently, so you know it's onto something.)

Kingfish

∽ DOPE ∽

"Dope" is a complimentary word used frequently to describe great cocktails (among other things) in New Orleans, and this drink—with its surprising combination of Galliano and smoky mezcal—certainly fits the bill.

Attributed to Christine Jeanine Nielsen at Angeline.

GLASSWARE: Double Old Fashioned glass
GARNISH: Grapefruit peel, expressed

- **1 whole egg**
- **1 oz mezcal, preferably Del Maguey Vida**
- **1 oz Galliano**
- **1 oz pineapple juice**
- **1 dash lactart**

TO ASSEMBLE:

1. In a cocktail tin, dry shake (see page 13) the egg and mezcal.

2. Add remaining ingredients and shake again.

3. Double strain into an Old Fashioned glass.

4. Express the oils of a grapefruit peel over the cocktail and discard.

AGUARDIENTE DOLAR

Vallet Amargo is an unusual, aubergine-hued apertivo. It's probably like nothing you've ever sampled before—especially when paired with cinnamon-infused mezcal and ginger syrup.
Attributed to Jesse Carr at Balise.

❦

GLASSWARE: Collins glass

GARNISH: Angostura bitters, lime wheel

- **1¾ oz cinnamon-infused mezcal, preferably Del Maguey Vida**
- **¼ oz Vallet Amargo liqueur**
- **¾ oz lime juice**
- **¾ oz ginger syrup**
- **Ginger ale, to top**

TO ASSEMBLE:

1. In a cocktail tin, combine all ingredients except ginger ale. Shake.

2. Strain into a Collins glass.

3. Top with ginger ale, 6 dashes Angostura, and a lime wheel, mounted.

❦

✦ **Ginger Syrup:** In a large pot, combine 1 cup finely minced ginger, 1 cup white sugar, and 3 cups water. Bring to a boil, then reduce heat to medium. Cook down until reduced by half and syrup is thick. Allow to cool, strain through cheese cloth into a clean bowl. Store in an airtight container in the refrigerator for 2 weeks.

✦ **Cinnamon-Infused Mezcal:** Place 4–5 3-inch cinnamon sticks inside the bottle of mezcal. Store in a cool, dry place, shaking daily, for 5 days. Taste. Store for 1 month.

BAR SPOTLIGHT

Sylvain

625 Chartres St
New Orleans, LA 70130
Phone: (504) 265-8123
www.sylvainnola.com

Sylvain is a testament to how, sometimes, the best things can come in small packages. The city's premiere gastropub (named after a one-act comic opera once performed in the French Quarter), Sylvain's dimly-lit, intimate interior is always boisterous and jam-packed with couples dressed to the nines and in-the-know locals looking for a night out on the town. The bar program is dedicated to crafting cocktails that are consistently stellar without falling into pretentious territory, and—in most weather—drinks are most enjoyable sipped in the restaurant's palm-shaded courtyard.

NO FUN

A kick of green chartreuse in tandem with a zippy strawberry shrub ensures that the No Fun is the kind of courtyard-perfect drink that's destined to be a bourbon-based, rousing good time—aka, lots of fun.

Attributed to Darrin Ylisto at Sylvain.

GLASSWARE: Rocks glass

GARNISH: None

- 1½ oz bourbon, preferably Buffalo Trace
- ½ oz green chartreuse
- ½ oz strawberry balsamic shrub
- ½ oz lemon juice

TO ASSEMBLE:

1. In a cocktail tin, combine all ingredients with ice. Shake.

✦ **Strawberry Balsamic Shrub:** In a large pot, add 2 pints halved strawberries with tops removed, 3 cups white sugar, and ½ cup water. Bring to a boil. Reduce heat to low and allow strawberries to soften, approximately 5 minutes. Add 2½ cups balsamic vinegar. Increase heat to medium-high and bring to a boil again. Once boiling, reduce heat to a simmer and skim the brown foam from the top. Allow to reduce slightly over low heat, approximately 10 minutes. Strain off strawberries and store shrub in airtight bottle.

⤳ ROLLO RAIDERS ⤳

Yogurt—no, not the fruit-on-the-bottom kind—meets the icy, Nordic bite of Aquavit and Kümmel (a caraway and fennel-flavored liqueur) in this surprisingly tangy, creamy concoction. *Attributed to Jesse Carr at Balise.*

GLASSWARE: Rocks glass
GARNISH: Two lemon peels, sprinkle of caraway seeds

- ¾ oz plain, full-fat yogurt
- ½ oz orgeat
- ¾ oz lemon juice
- ¾ oz aquavit
- ¾ oz kümmel
- ½ oz gin, preferably Beefeater

TO ASSEMBLE:

1. In a cocktail tin, combine all ingredients and short shake (see page 14).

2. Double strain into a rocks glass filled with crushed ice.

3. Garnish with two lemon peels and a sprinkle of caraway seeds.

❧ CROSS-EYED AND PAINLESS ❧

Cleverly named after a Talking Heads song, this cocktail reimagines the reaches of sloe gin by pairing it with tequila and curaçao.

Attributed to the Ace Hotel.

GLASSWARE: Coupe glass

GARNISH: Lemon twist

- ¾ oz sloe gin
- ¾ oz tequila
- ¾ oz dry curaçao
- ¾ oz Lillet Rouge
- 1 dash Angostura bitters
- ⅛ oz Herbsaint

TO ASSEMBLE:

1. In a mixing glass, combine all ingredients except Herbsaint. Stir.

2. Add Herbsaint to a coupe glass, swirl to coat, and dump excess.

3. Strain mixing glass contents into coupe.

4. Garnish with a lemon twist.

COMPÉRE LAPIN

The Old No. 77 Hotel & Chandlery
535 Tchoupitoulas St
New Orleans, LA 70130
Phone: (504) 599-2119
www.comperelapin.com

There's a lot to love about the edible fare at Compére Lapin in the Warehouse District, where St. Lucian-born chef Nina Compton (of Top Chef fame) serves up Caribbean delicacies from conch fritters to crispy pig ears.

Bartender Spotlight

At Compére Lapin's rabbit-adorned bar, though, the draw is the effervescent Abigail Gullo, whose vivacious personality means she can often be found singing and dancing while whipping up cocktails. Originally from Hyde Park, New York, Abigail might not be a native New Orleanian, but the city is clearly where she's meant to be. With a flower adorning her hair and her K9 sidekick, Ronnie Magic, never too far away, she is downright radiant behind the bar, glowing with the same kind of joie de vivre that can be found from trumpet solos in the Treme to two-stepping in nearby Cajun country. She's a natural.

ON ABIGAIL'S FAVORITE PLACES TO GO WHEN NOT WORKING:

"Pagoda Cafe and Satsuma are both perfect for tasty food, coffee, and doggie play dates. I am also obsessed with the stuffed bagels at Cake Cafe. During crawfish season, I love to go to Bucktown to pick up some hot crawfish and eat it by the lake."

⌒ CHARBONNEAU WAY ⌒

The Charbonneau Way is an homage to Abigail Gullo's French-Canadian roots and is named after the road where her family had a maple syrup-making sugar house.

Attributed to Abigail Gullo at Compére Lapin.

GLASSWARE: Coupe glass

GARNISH: Fresh thyme

- **2 oz rye whiskey**
- **½ oz lemon**
- **½ oz maple syrup**
- **¼ oz Suze**
- **Absinthe, for misting**

TO ASSEMBLE:

1. In a cocktail tin, combine all ingredients with ice. Shake.

2. Strain into a coupe that has been misted with absinthe (see page 13).

3. Garnish with a sprig of fresh thyme.

E. J. HART & Co
IMPORTERS
WHOLESALE
DRUGGISTS & GROCERS
DRUGS * CHEMICALS
Window Glass

⤙ GENTLEMAN CALLER ⤚

A sherry cocktail that pulls no punches about being spirit-forward, this is the kind of drink ideal for serving up when an unexpected (but very welcome) guest arrives on your doorstep. *Attributed to Abigail Gullo at Compére Lapin.*

⚜

GLASSWARE: Nick and Nora glass

GARNISH: Lemon peel

- **1 oz gin**
- **1 oz fino sherry**
- **½ oz Aperol**
- **½ oz génépy**
- **4 drops Bittermens Burlesque Bitters**

TO ASSEMBLE:

1. In a mixing glass, combine all ingredients. Stir.

2. Strain into a Nick & Nora glass.

3. Garnish with a lemon peel.

ON ABIGAIL'S DEEP LOVE OF SHERRY, AND WHY NEW ORLEANS IS THE PERFECT PLACE FOR ITS CONTINUED REVIVAL:

"New Orleans is a French city with Spanish architecture. Our lifestyle of relaxed reverence for drinking and food is very Spanish, indeed. Sherry is a wine made to go with food. The dry sherry in particular is so refreshing, and goes great with seafood. It's perfect for our climate and cuisine."

ON ABIGAIL'S MOST MEMORABLE NEW ORLEANS NIGHT BEHIND THE BAR:

"I had these delightful young men at the bar one night. When I presented them with their cocktails, one guy exclaimed, 'You just did a drum solo on my face!' Turns out, they were in a band playing around the corner at the House of Blues. They were so sweet, and gave me free tickets to the show. Serving them and then having them serve up some rock—in my face—a few hours later was pretty cool. I still send Mardi Gras beads to their kids."

Guaranteed to be a drum-solo-to-the-face experience. *Attributed to Abigail Gullo at Compére Lapin.*

GLASSWARE: Collins glass

GARNISH: Grapefruit peel, expressed

- **1 oz Scotch**
- **¾ oz Campari**
- **¾ oz lemon juice**

- **½ oz honey syrup**
- **3 oz dry French pear cider**

TO ASSEMBLE:

1. In a cocktail tin, combine all ingredients except cider. Shake.

2. Strain into a tall Collins glass with ice.

3. Top with pear cider, and express a grapefruit peel over the top for garnish.

✦ **Honey Syrup:** In a small saucepan, combine 1 cup local honey with ½ cup water over medium heat. Stir until thinned and completely combined. Store in an airtight container for up to 2 weeks in the refrigerator.

BAMBOO ROAD: NEW
ORLEANS' TIKI CULTURE

New Orleans wears its unofficial title of the "Northernmost Caribbean City" with the utmost pride, from the subtropical climate and summer squalls to the Creole flavors found on plates and in glasses. Naturally, tiki drinks fit right in, with their homage to freshness and frivolity making them ideal warm weather concoctions.

Recently, New Orleans has blasted past the syrupy, trop-rock indulgences of Bourbon Street (Hand Grenade, anyone?) and ridden the wave of modern tiki revival with decided aplomb. The city has assembled a triple threat known loosely as the city's "Tiki Main Street" along Decatur in the French Quarter.

Of course, tiki's influence can be found almost everywhere across the city. It wouldn't surprise anyone to hear that some of New Orleans' finest barkeeps dream of simply dipping further south when they retire to open seaside shacks, pouring beers on the white sands until the sun sets.

"EVERYONE IN THIS GOOD CITY ENJOYS
THE FULL RIGHT TO PURSUE HIS OWN
INCLINATIONS IN ALL REASONABLE AND
UNREASONABLE WAYS."

—*The Daily Picayune, 1851*

LATITUDE 29

321 N Peters St
New Orleans, LA 70130
Phone: (504) 609-3811
www.latitude29nola.com

Operated by tiki mastermind and modern-day trailblazer Jeff "Beachbum" Berry, Latitude 29 is a tribute to the luau scholar's decades of experience unearthing long-dormant recipes from the coffers of Trader Vic and Donn the Beachcomber.

"New Orleans was part of the Golden Age of Tiki, from the 1930s through the 1970s: the days after Prohibition to the dawn of disco," says Berry.

At Latitude, drinks like the Pontchartrain Pearl Diver and the Niu Niu blend tiki's surf-happy past and creativity-driven present together with a special New Orleans flourish.

"What they were doing [with tiki drinks] was craft cocktails," says Berry. "They were doing culinary craft cocktails decades before these terms came into existence. What Latitude is trying to do is reconnect tiki with this wonderful craft cocktail renaissance that we've had and to sort of make the point that they're not mutually exclusive.

For Berry, New Orleans is the ideal city to base his international tiki empire. "We felt like, okay, we're not in the U.S., we are in the Republic of New Orleans," laughs Berry.

HAVING A DRINK WITH...

JEFF "BEACHBUM" BERRY OF LATITUDE 29

Mention the words "tiki drink" and one name automatically springs to mind: Jeff "Beachbum" Berry. The country's foremost tiki scholar and co-owner of Latitude 29, Berry's charm and enthusiasm for the entire tiki ethos is nothing short of infectious.

SB: What inspired you to make the move to New Orleans and open Latitude 29?

JB: Why New Orleans? That has a lot to do with Tales of the Cocktail. [My wife] Annene and I had never been to New Orleans before 2005, but we were looking for a place to move to from Los Angeles. There wasn't any city in the country that was doing it for us. Then we got invited to Tales [in 2005], stepped off the shuttle in the French Quarter, and it was like, "Where the hell has this place been all of our lives? " We felt like we weren't in the United States anymore, which was awesome. Everybody was just incredibly cool and helpful and encouraging. This town was where the love was, plus, it didn't have a tiki bar.

SB: Tiki demigod Donn the Beachcomber has long been rumored to be from New Orleans. What's the real story?

JB: Up until very recently, I had heard that Donn the Beach-comber was born in New Orleans. So, moving here was like this full circle thing. The guy who singlehandedly invented the tiki bar and the tiki drink in 1934 was a New Orleanian, and we were bringing his drinks back. A lot of the drinks on our menu are Donn the Beachcomber drinks. Everybody stole from Donn, and he was sort of the big bang. But I've since found out from David Wondrich—the man who spoils everybody's favorite cocktail legends—that Donn was born in Mexia, Texas, but his parents were from New Orleans.

SB: Close enough, I think! In your mind, what does the ideal tiki bar look like?

JB: At tiki bars you generally get two out of three things. The trifecta—good food, good drinks, and good atmosphere—is really hard to get. I always found that I would get two out of three at best. The Mai-Kai in Ft. Lauderdale was one of the few that delivered all three. It's still there actually. What we really strived to do—with a much more limited budget and trying to use our imaginations—was to deliver on all those three accounts. I was pretty confident about the drinks, but it took [my wife] Annene working with our chef to really come up with food that paired well with the drinks and worked independently of them as well. That's one thing I love about it. Then, of course, for me the atmosphere was very important. You can't have a tiki bar without an immersive atmosphere. Otherwise, why even bother? I see a lot of places opening up, and they just look like your basic 1920s bar but they're serving tiki food? Sorry, that's not good enough. You haven't committed yet.

SB: I think you've hit all three out of the park.

MOLOKAI MISHAP

Cocchi Americano is an Italian apertivo best known for being a key ingredient in the Corpse Reviver #2. In the Molokai Mishap, it helps create a seaside-ready sipper perfect for an afternoon of beachy dreams.

Attributed to Brad Smith at Latitude 29.

GLASSWARE: Double Old Fashioned glass
GARNISH: None

- **1 oz Cocchi Americano**
- **1 oz peach liqueur, preferably Rothman & Winter**
- **1 oz pineapple juice**
- **1 oz white rhum agricole**
- **8 drops Bittermens Elemakule Tiki Bitters**

TO ASSEMBLE:

1. In a double Old Fashioned glass, combine all ingredients over two large ice cubes. Stir.

SEA BEAST

Fernet—the bitter Italian spirit—isn't a spirit typically associated with tiki drinks, but finds balance here from the acidity of the lime and passion fruit's juiciness.

Attributed to Brad Smith at Latitude 29.

GLASSWARE: Highball glass

GARNISH: None

- ¾ oz lime juice
- ¾ oz passion fruit purée
- ¾ oz fernet
- 1 oz Rhum Clément Sirop de Canne, can substitute a rich simple syrup
- 1½ oz rum, preferably Clement VSOP

TO ASSEMBLE:

1. In a cocktail tin filled with ice, combine all ingredients. Shake.

2. Strain into highball glass filled with cubed ice.

CANE & TABLE

1113 Decatur St
New Orleans, LA 70116
Phone: (504) 581-1112
www.caneandtablenola.com

Cane & Table is the city's "proto-tiki" pioneer, working to push the limits of the genre's past, present, and future. Co-owner and consummate rum nerd Nick Detrich leads this wonky-meets-delicious charge, fueled by his downright encyclopedic knowledge of boozy Caribbean history. Each drink fuses together flavor combinations that may seem quirky on paper (like a play on the Sazerac made with spruce bitters) but possess inspired levels of depth.

Always on the cutting edge of what's up and coming, Detrich believes the following four ingredients will be the next big thing in the world of island-inspired beverages:

WHITE GRAPEFRUIT "I hope that we will see more demand for white grapefruits when they're in season. Other grapefruits are all products of the mid-twentieth century, but the white grapefruit was called for in many early tiki drinks. If part of tiki's allure is that it traces a narrative from the tropics to our neighborhood, then the path of the grapefruit is the perfect encapsulation of that story."

FALERNUM "Yes, it has always been around to a certain degree, but it's the most underrated ingredient in tiki with the finest pedigree (outside of rum, of course). The earliest it has been dated back to is 1703 by the folks at Mount Gay Rum [in Barbados], but it probably extends further back than that. It became popular in the first tiki drinks—Zombie, Royal Bermuda Yacht Club—but is noticeably absent in later drinks."

WORMWOOD BITTERS "Many tiki ingredients seek drying agents (absinthe, for instance) in order to mitigate the many syrups and richer rums. Wormwood bitters were used in just such a way in the islands, but never made their way to the tiki movement."

RAISINS AND RAISIN-ADJACENT FLAVORS (CREAM SHERRY, RAISIN-INFUSED LIQUEURS, ETC.) "You'll find raisins used in many mid-nineteenth century recipes for various cordials, syrups, and infusions to add rich and nutty notes to punches and spirits. Today, you will still find a good number of raisin infused rum cordials that will probably make landfall in the United States soon."

~ ABSENT STARS ~

This bitter-meets-fruity-meets-salty concoction speaks to just how complex and delicious magenta, tiki-adjacent drinks can taste. In order to craft the saline solution, simply dissolve two teaspoons of sea salt in four ounces of water.

Attributed to Nick Detrich at Cane & Table.

GLASSWARE: Double Old Fashioned glass

GARNISH: Expressed orange twist

- 1 oz Campari
- 1 oz white rhum agricole, preferably La Favorite Blanc
- ¾ oz lemon juice
- ½ oz passion fruit syrup
- ½ oz apricot brandy, preferably Marie Brizard Apry
- 5 drops saline
- 10 drops Bittermens Hopped Grapefruit Bitters

TO ASSEMBLE:

1. In a cocktail tin half-filled with ice, combine all ingredients. Shake approximately 20 times.

2. Strain into a chilled double Old Fashioned glass filled with ice.

3. Rub the rim of the glass with an orange twist, then mount.

BOSS COLADA

One of Cane & Table's most popular and eye-catching drinks, the Boss Colada is a sunshine-laden sipper accessible to even the least likely rum connoisseur. If you're feeling frisky and bat your eyelashes just right, ask for it to be served in a freshly cut pineapple or secret whale-shaped glass.

Attributed to Nick Detrich at Cane & Table.

GLASSWARE: Footed pilsner
GARNISH: Peychaud's bitters, lime wheel

- **1 oz Bittermens Bäska Snaps**
- **½ oz rum, preferably Banks 7**
- **1½ oz pineapple juice**
- **½ oz lime juice**
- **½ oz orgeat**

TO ASSEMBLE:

1. In a cocktail tin, combine all ingredients and shake brusquely for about 10 seconds.

2. Strain into a footed pilsner glass filled with pebble ice.

3. Drizzle 3 dashes of Peychaud's over top of the drink, and mount a lime wheel on the side.

White grapefruit juice is delightfully more acidic than pink and an original classic tiki ingredient. This cocktail spotlights how grapefruit can play nice with an unusual partner—smoky, peaty Scotch.

Attributed to Nick Detrich at Cane & Table.

GLASSWARE: Double Old Fashioned glass
GARNISH: Orange peel

- **1½ oz Scotch, preferably Monkey Shoulder**
- **¾ oz Cocchi Americano**
- **¾ oz Cocchi Vermouth di Torino**

- **½ oz white grapefruit juice**
- **4 drops smoked salt tincture**

TO ASSEMBLE:

1. In a double Old Fashioned glass, combine all ingredients. Stir.

2. Garnish with orange peel.

✦ **Smoked Salt Tincture:** In a small bowl, dissolve 2 teaspoons hickory-smoked salt in 4 ounces water.

TIKI TOLTECA

301 N Peters St
New Orleans, LA 70130
Phone: (504) 581-1112
www.tikitolteca.com

Located in the crow's nest above a French Quarter Mexican restaurant and anchoring one end of New Orleans' Tiki Row, Tiki Tolteca is the ultimate in kitschy fun—right down to the Hawaiian print shirts and crooning sounds of Don Ho. The tiki gummies are a particularly playful menu item, with chewy (but no less boozy) versions of a Hurricane, Mai Tai, and Zombie molded in the shape of tiki gods. If you've been waiting for Jell-O shots to make a return, think of these as a more "adult" iteration.

A classic crowd pleaser that will leave you wanting a second (and third), the What A Aspirin Is goes down maybe a little too easily.

Attributed to Tiki Tolteca.

GLASSWARE: Tiki mug or Collins glass

GARNISH: Orange slice, cinnamon stick, freshly grated nutmeg

- **2½ oz dark rum**
- **1 oz cream of coconut, preferably Coco Lopez**
- **1 oz orange juice**
- **4 oz pineapple juice**

TO ASSEMBLE:

1. In a cocktail tin filled with crushed ice, combine all ingredients. Shake.

2. Pour into a large tiki mug or Collins glass and fill with ice to top.

3. Garnish with an orange slice, cinnamon stick, and freshly grated nutmeg.

INSIDER'S CHOICE: WHERE
BARTENDERS DRINK

BAR TONIQUE

New Orleans is a 24-hour kind of town, and with that comes a wide swath of late-night watering holes popular with the city's bartenders post-shift. While these places typically serve beers, shots, and straight spirits versus complicated cocktails, they're the perfect spots for anyone—bartender or not—looking to wind down after a long night.

"HISTORY IS MARBLE, AND REMAINS FOREVER COLD, EVEN UNDER THE MOST ARTISTIC HAND, UNLESS LIFE IS BREATHED INTO IT BY THE IMAGINATION."

—Charles Gayarré, historian and writer from New Orleans, in Aubert Dubayet: Or the Two Sister Republics, 1882

BAR SPOTLIGHT

BAR TONIQUE
820 N Rampart St
New Orleans, LA 70116
Phone: (504) 324-6045
www.bartonique.com

If a person works in or around cocktails in New Orleans, they'll definitely have a story (or seven) to tell about late nights at Bar Tonique.

"I think we're a more unique bar than perhaps we ought to be, or than perhaps you might think we'd be," says Mark Schettler, the bar manager at Tonique. "We're a small, divey neighborhood joint serving a rough-around-the-edges, off-the-beaten-path area of the French Quarter. We have a very strong service industry following, and because of that, have always been known as a bar that goes late."

Very late, in fact. I once stayed until way past my bedtime and promptly missed a 6:00 a.m. work flight the

next morning. (Whoops.) It's easy to lose track of time simply because, well, everyone at Tonique is always having so much damn
fun that it's downright contagious. But the bar isn't a typical, beer-
and-a-shot dive by any means: it walks a tightrope between cocktail culture and neighborhood joint with a drink on each arm for
balance.

"Our cocktail program has a menu that's something like 12 pages
long—and forever being stolen—we easily go through a handful a
day!" Schettler laughs. "We serve almost all pre-prohibition classics, and the bartenders are expected to know a lot more than
just what's on the list. We're a no-frills, no pretension, operation
that focuses on letting our bartenders' talents shine through, and
the bartenders just happen to keep on kicking ass at their jobs
every single day."

⌣ TONIQUE'S SAZERAC ⌣

Tonique's glassware only comes in three sizes—short, medium, or tall—but an Old Fashioned glass will do the trick for this drink. Gomme syrup is a style of simple syrup made with gum arabic that works to smooth out the cocktail's texture, making it super silky, so take extra time to enjoy the drink's full mouthfeel.
Attributed to Tonique's.

GLASSWARE: Old Fashioned glass

GARNISH: Expressed lemon twist

- ⅛ oz Herbsaint
- 2 oz rye whiskey
- ¼ oz gomme syrup
- 9 dashes Peychaud's bitters

TO ASSEMBLE:

1. Coat the inside of a chilled Old Fashioned glass with Herbsaint, discard excess.

2. In a cocktail tin with ice, stir remaining ingredients and strain into prepared glass.

3. Express oils of lemon twist over glass and mount to garnish.

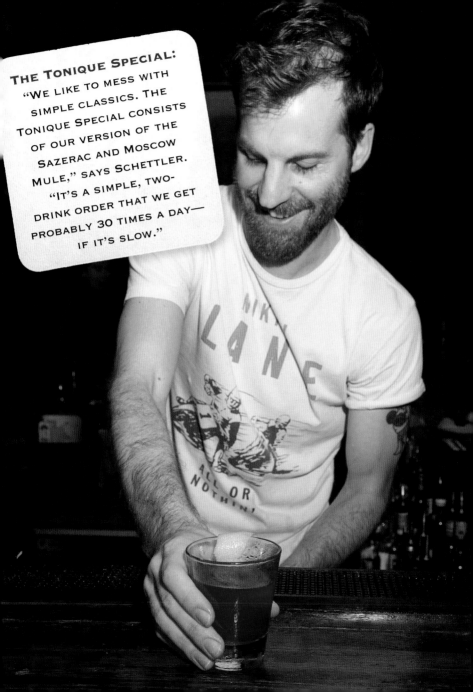

THE TONIQUE SPECIAL: "WE LIKE TO MESS WITH SIMPLE CLASSICS. THE TONIQUE SPECIAL CONSISTS OF OUR VERSION OF THE SAZERAC AND MOSCOW MULE," SAYS SCHETTLER. "IT'S A SIMPLE, TWO-DRINK ORDER THAT WE GET PROBABLY 30 TIMES A DAY— IF IT'S SLOW."

MOSCOW MULE

With a mouth-puckering brightness and a burst of bold, fresh ginger syrup, one sip of this zippy second-wind-in-a-glass and you'll be able to go a little longer into the wee small hours of the morning. Whether or not that's a good idea, of course, is another story entirely.

Attributed to Tonique's.

GLASSWARE: Collins glass

GARNISH: None

- **2 oz vodka**
- **½ oz lemon juice**
- **½ oz lime juice**
- **½ oz ginger syrup**
- **½ oz rich simple syrup**
- **2 oz soda water**

To Assemble:

1. In a glass half-filled with ice, combine all ingredients. Stir gently.

✦ **Ginger Syrup:** Combine 1 cup finely minced ginger, 1 cup granulated sugar, and 3 cups water. Bring to a boil, then reduce to medium heat. Cook down until reduced by half and the syrup is thick enough to coat the back of a spoon. Allow to cool and strain through cheesecloth into a clean bowl. Store in an airtight container for up to 1 week.

BAR SPOTLIGHT

BARREL PROOF

1201 Magazine St
New Orleans, LA 70130
Phone: (504) 299-1888
www.barrelproofnola.com

It's hard to find a time the dark, sprawling space at Barrel Proof isn't teeming with post-shift bartenders and whiskey-lovers spilling out into the street. Anchoring a wide corner on the edge of the Lower Garden District, the bar boasts the finest collection of brown liquor—ryes, bourbons, and whiskeys of all shapes and sizes—in New Orleans, but also has a stellar beer list and the ability to whip up cocktails on the fly.

CRANBERRY SHANDY

A handful of the bartenders at Barrel Proof and I have a special fondness for a certain cranberry-flavored ready-to-drink beverage. Late one night, bartender Thomas Thompson attempted to craft his own, fresh version for us. The Cranberry Shandy below was the tart, delicious end result.

GLASSWARE: Pilsner glass
GARNISH: None

- **2 oz cranberry shandy syrup**
- **12 oz beer, preferably an IPA**

TO ASSEMBLE:

1. In a pilsner glass, mix syrup and beer.

2. Stir gently until combined.

✦ **Cranberry Shandy Syrup:** In a small saucepan, combine 12 ounces fresh cranberries, 1½ cups water, ¾ cup white sugar, ¼ cup lime juice, and 1 lemon peel and bring to a boil over medium-high heat. After mixture begins to boil, reduce heat to a simmer and stir continuously with a wooden spoon, gently pressing the cranberries against the sides of the pot until they have all broken down. Once the mixture has reduced by half, remove from heat. Strain through cheesecloth into a large bowl. Allow to cool, and refrigerate in an airtight container for up to 1 week.

BELOVED DIVES

BROTHERS III

Neighborhood: Uptown
4520 Magazine St
New Orleans, LA 70115
Phone: (504) 897-9912

A low-slung, mustard-colored building with a country-western jukebox and legions of dedicated day drinkers, Brothers III is a 24-hour dive best visited after you've had a couple elsewhere.

CROWN & ANCHOR

Neighborhood: Algiers Point
200 Pelican Ave
New Orleans, LA 70114
Phone: (504) 227-1007

Located a ferry-ride across the river in the Westbank neighborhood of Algiers Point, Crown & Anchor has a community vibe that will immediately make you feel like an insider and British trappings that ensure lagers and chips are in strong supply.

ERIN ROSE

Neighborhood: French Quarter
811 Conti St
New Orleans, LA 70112
Phone: (504) 522-3573

A service industry favorite in the French Quarter known for their cure-for-what-ails-you frozen Irish coffee, you can't leave Erin Rose without snagging a bite to-go from Killer Poboys, the inventive, Vietnamese-inspired po'boy shop in the back of the bar.

KAJUN'S

Neighborhood: Bywater
2256 St Claude Ave
New Orleans, LA 70117
Phone: (504) 947-3735

Kajun's is the finest karaoke dive in the city, where everyone is encouraged to get in on the act. Be prepared to see things here you didn't know were possible, like wedding proposals to the sounds of Meatloaf and septuagenarian rap performances.

THE SAINT

Neighborhood: Lower Garden District
961 St Mary St
New Orleans, LA 70130
Phone: (504) 523-0050

A shot and a beer is standard fare at this immensely popular, punk-driven Lower Garden District dive, where "Tikioke Tuesday" might be the only place in the world where this much metal meets Blue Hawaii.

SNAKE AND JAKE'S

Neighborhood: Uptown
7612 Oak St
New Orleans, LA 70118
Phone: (504) 861-2802

Perhaps the most legendary of all New Orleans dive bars, Snake and Jake's is nestled in an Uptown neighborhood and frequented by everyone from celebrities to old-timers to college kids from nearby Tulane. If you're venturing out that way, be prepared to stay out until the sun comes up in the red-lit room: There's no such thing as "one drink" here.

LEGENDARY DIVE: NICK'S BIG TRAIN BAR

Neighborhood: Tulane Avenue
Permanently Closed

Nick's Big Train Bar was, by all accounts, the city's finest example of a neighborhood joint, where Dixie Beer flowed freely and the longtime owner claimed to have created the world's largest Café Pousse (a multi-layered, multi-colored stacked cocktail). Tragically, the bar (and Dixie Beer) was lost during Hurricane Katrina, but plans to rebuild are currently in the works.

SPIKE IT: REIMAGINING
MILK AND COFFEE

Milk and coffee are, for the most part, pretty innocent: We drink them apart and together, to wake up and go to sleep. (Let she who hasn't enjoyed a glass of warm bedtime milk be the first to judge.) Most of the time, these elementary ingredients stay away from the liquor cabinet, happy to live as foils to our more devilish vices.

In New Orleans, though, things are a little bit different. Tradition insists that liquor-infused after-dinner coffees and boozy daybreak milks are a way of life, ensuring that from sunrise to sunset, there's a little bit of cocktail-fueled pep in your step.

"THE BIRD THAT WOULD SOAR ABOVE THE LEVEL PLAIN OF TRADITION AND PREJUDICE MUST HAVE STRONG WINGS."

—*Kate Chopin, in The Awakening, 1899, set in New Orleans*

∽ LITTLE BLACK STAR ∽

Named after a song by local indie-rock band Hurray for the Riff Raff and served at Cuban bar El Libre, this cold coffee-based concoction feels like the perfect jolt of energy after indulging in a heat-induced afternoon siesta.

Attributed to Bazil Zerinsky at Catahoula/El Libre.

GLASSWARE: Coupe glass

GARNISH: Star anise pod

- 1½ oz rum, preferably Treaty Oak Barrel Reserve
- ½ oz coffee syrup
- ½ oz fresh lime juice
- ¼ oz curaçao, preferably Pierre Ferrand
- ⅛ oz maraschino liqueur

To Assemble:

1. In a cocktail tin, combine all ingredients. Shake.

2. Strain into a coupe and garnish with star anise pod.

✦ **Coffee Syrup:** In a small saucepan, combine 2 cups sugar, 1 cup water, 2¼ ounces espresso, preferably Bustelo, 1 dash cinnamon, and 1 dash chili powder and bring to a boil. Reduce heat to medium, stirring until the mixture coats the back of a spoon. Store in an airtight container for up to 1 week.

~ FROZEN COOKIE MILK PUNCH ~

"**B**runches in New Orleans are nothing without milk punches," says Meagan Burke, bartender at F & B Department and to whom this drink is attributed to. "Made with brandy, bourbon, or the occasional splash of rum, these creamy saviors have endless variations." In her own spin, Burke creates a brandy-fueled milk punch that could easily double as a quick-fix dessert.

GLASSWARE: Collins glass
GARNISH: Chocolate shavings
YIELD: 2 cocktails

- **2 cups vanilla ice cream**
- **4 medium chocolate chip cookies, broken into pieces**
- **3 oz cognac**

TO ASSEMBLE:

1. In a blender, combine all ingredients and blend until smooth and incorporated. (Want it thicker? Add more ice cream. Want it thinner? Add more booze.)

2. Garnish with chocolate shavings and serve immediately.

ᕙ BRANDY MILK PUNCH ᕘ

A staple of Mardi Gras mornings for those looking to feel simultaneously calcium-fortified and liquored up, brandy milk punch has found particular acclaim at Galatoire's, the gilded Grand Dame where leisurely three-hour Friday lunches worth waiting in line for are de rigueur. If you prefer bourbon to brandy, feel free to sub it in.

GLASSWARE: Wine glass

GARNISH: Freshly grated nutmeg

- **3 oz whole milk**
- **1 oz half-and-half**
- **2 oz brandy**
- **1 oz simple syrup (see page 14)**
- **½ teaspoon vanilla extract**

TO ASSEMBLE:

1. In a cocktail tin, combine all ingredients. Shake.

2. Strain into a chilled wine glass.

3. Garnish with freshly grated nutmeg.

CARIBBEAN MILK PUNCH

Brennan's famous Caribbean Milk Punch speaks to this intersection of classic and contemporary, adding rum and fresh vanilla bean to the mix for a more island-inspired start to the day. *Attributed to Brennan's.*

GLASSWARE: Coupe glass

GARNISH: Freshly grated nutmeg

- **1 oz rum, preferably Smith and Cross or Mt. Gay Black Barrel**
- **½ oz bourbon, preferably Buffalo Trace**
- **1 oz vanilla bean-infused simple syrup**
- **1 oz heavy cream**

TO ASSEMBLE:

1. In a cocktail tin with ice, combine all ingredients. Shake until frothy.

2. Strain into a coupe with no ice.

3. Garnish with freshly grated nutmeg.

✦ **Vanilla Bean Infused Simple Syrup:** In a small sauce pan, combine 1 cup sugar and 1 cup water and bring to a boil over medium-high heat. Cut one vanilla bean in half lengthwise and scrape seeds from the pod. Add pod and seeds to syrup mixture and reduce to a simmer, until mixture coats the back of a spoon. Remove from heat, allow to cool, and store in an airtight glass jar in the refrigerator for up to 2 weeks.

BRENNAN'S

417 Royal St
New Orleans, LA 70130
Phone: (504) 525-9711
www.brennansneworleans.com

With its signature flamingo-pink exterior and recent, breathtaking renovation, Brennan's is a French Quarter stalwart committed to maintaining its legacy with a modern edge.

"The one thing that we really wanted to do was to just make sure that at the end of the day, we had good cocktails. We knew that we were never going to be the place that had a thousand different tinctures, and we always have to have a nod to the traditional," says Joe Billebach, Brennan's beverage director. "It was more about making sure that we're using the best ingredients."

Indeed, the bar has made it easy for guests to play it safe and experiment in equal measure, thanks to programs like the Build-Your-Own Sazerac Project.

"We knew we had to do a classic one, but we wanted to do something where people could maybe build their own," says Billebach. "The initial idea was that we have the basic one, then a little nicer rye where it has a different expression, and then we'd have that wildcard option. Right now, we have a clear rye we're trying out. It's this idea that you can create your own experience, and it gives you something a little bit more nuanced."

CAFÉ BRULOT

A veritable three-ring circus of fire and showmanship, Café Brulot (or, as it is sometimes known, Café Brulot Diabolique) has been an after-dinner spectacle entertaining giddy diners fresh off multi-course meals for more than a century. Elegant, old-line restaurant Antoine's lays claim to its creation (c. 1890), with the drink's popularity spiking during Prohibition as coffee and citrus notes proved to be an expert disguise for the brandy-based sins within. The Café Brulot is so special and wildly over-the-top that—in a restaurant setting—it requires its own unique equipment, the Brulot bowl, to complete the flame-shooting, tableside production. At home, the fire is (thankfully) a bit more contained, and ready for your attempts in the recipe below. If nothing else, Café Brulot is the kind of big, brassy diva cocktail that will leave you yearning for one more as the spice-notes settle and the brandy hits when you least expect it.

GLASSWARE: Demitasse cups
GARNISH: Long orange peel
YIELD: 6 servings

- 1½ oz brandy
- 1½ oz orange liqueur, preferably Cointreau
- 2 3-inch cinnamon sticks
- 6 cloves

- 2 star anise pods
- 1 2-inch lemon peel
- 1 2-inch orange peel
- 1 teaspoon granulated sugar
- 3 cups hot brewed coffee

To Assemble:

1. In a heatproof bowl, combine all ingredients except coffee and warm over an open flame.

2. When the brandy is hot, but not boiling, carefully transfer to the table and ignite using a long fireplace match. The mixture will flame, then cool.

3. After flame has extinguished, stir gently using a ladle, then pour hot coffee into brandy mixture. Stir until combined.

4. Ladle mixture into demitasse cups or teacups and garnish with a long orange peel.

⤸ CHAI TODDY ⤷

This Chai Toddy is simple to assemble but surprisingly punchy for those who prefer tea to coffee and a powerful stroke of spice.

GLASSWARE: Teacup

GARNISH: None

- **6 oz chai tea concentrate**
- **2 oz bourbon, preferably Knob Creek**
- **Splash hot water**

TO ASSEMBLE:

1. In a tea kettle, steam chai according to package instructions.

2. In a teacup or coffee mug, add bourbon and then pour chai over top.

3. Add a splash of hot water.

 REDEFINING THE NEIGHBORHOOD
BAR AT CURE

Ask almost any tippler in New Orleans, and they'll quickly tell you that almost no bar has helped to rebuild a New Orleans neighborhood more than Cure.

In the aftermath of Hurricane Katrina, neighborhood bars became critical meeting points for people to gather, share, and begin the rebuilding process. While already-established watering holes were the spots where neighbors started to pick up the pieces, new bars worked to help put the puzzle back together.

The passion project of Neal Bodenheimer and Kirk Estopinal, Cure (a 2016 James Beard finalist) was largely a destination location when it poured its first drinks on Freret Street in 2009, but steadily became a focal point around which the entire thoroughfare was reborn.

Today, the renovated 1905 fire station—with its soaring, floor-to-ceiling back bar, flora-drenched courtyard, and museum-like glass-case entryway filled with rare bottles and historic neighborhood treasures—is an always-buzzing nucleus of local activity.

Cure also worked to usher in a new era of innovative, envelope-pushing cocktail creation in the city, the likes of which was still a rarity at the time. The bar has nurtured some of the city's most talented drink-makers, working to create an ever-branching family tree of new bars across town equally committed to moving forward as to craft cocktail renaissance, while honoring the city's longstanding drinking traditions.

A classic in the Cure cannon (and one of my favorite drinks in the city), the Drink of Laughter and Forgetting dances between bitter and herbal with ingenious dexterity, thanks to the interplay between green chartreuse and cynar.

Attributed to Mike Yusko, formerly of Cure.

GLASSWARE: Cocktail glass

GARNISH: Angostura bitters

- 1½ oz cynar
- ½ oz green chartreuse
- ¾ oz lime
- ½ oz rich demerara syrup (see page 13, under rich simple syrup)
- 14 drops Angostura bitters

TO ASSEMBLE:

1. In a cocktail tin with ice, combine all ingredients. Shake.

2. Strain into a cocktail glass.

3. Garnish with a spray of Angostura bitters by filling a small, travel-sized spray bottle with Angostura bitters and spraying once over the drink.

BERLIN IN THE '70S

The Berlin in the '70s is a study in how kissing cousin ingredients—mezcal and tequila, lemon, and orange—can play nicely together, creating a sunny drink that warms from the inside out. *Billy Dollard, formerly of Cure.*

GLASSWARE: Coupe glass

GARNISH: Half an orange wheel, Fee Brothers Old Fashioned Bitters

- **1 oz mezcal, preferably Don Amado**
- **1 oz tequila, preferably Cabeza Blanco**
- **1 oz orange juice**
- **½ oz lemon juice**
- **½ oz cinnamon syrup**

TO ASSEMBLE:

1. In a cocktail tin with ice, combine all ingredients. Shake.

2. Strain into a double Old Fashioned glass.

3. Garnish with one dash of Old Fashioned bitters and mount half an orange wheel.

✦ **Cinnamon Syrup:** In a small saucepan, combine 1 cup water, 1 cup white sugar, and 4 3-inch cinnamon sticks. Bring to a boil over medium-high heat, then reduce to medium heat. When mixture has thickened, remove from heat and allow to cool. Remove cinnamon sticks and strain into an airtight container. Store, refrigerated, for up to 2 weeks.

⤳ THE HARDEST WALK ⤳

This cocktail flips the notion of the rum Old Fashioned on its head, inverting ingredient ratios to make vermouth the star while spotlighting how rum—in all its complexity—can make a fine supporting cast member for its bitter counterparts.

Attributed to Turk Dietrich at Cure.

GLASSWARE: Double Old Fashioned glass

GARNISH: Orange twist

- **2 oz punt e mes vermouth, preferably Carpano**
- **1 oz overproof rum, preferably Plantation**
- **½ teaspoon Gran Classico Bitter**
- **14 drops orange bitters, preferably Regan's**

TO ASSEMBLE:

1. In a mixing glass, combine all ingredients with ice and stir for about 30 revolutions.

2. Strain into a double Old Fashioned glass.

3. Garnish with an orange twist.

The star of this show is the pepita orgeat, which makes the traditional orgeat richer and more buttery, thanks to the pumpkin seeds. The drink is still stellar with regular orgeat.
Attributed to Neal Bodenheimer at Cure.

GLASSWARE: Double Old Fashioned glass
GARNISH: Mint top

- 1½ oz mezcal, preferably El Buho
- ½ oz añejo tequila, preferably Siembra Azul
- ¾ oz pepita orgeat
- ¾ oz lime juice
- 3 drops orange flower water
- 2 mint leaves
- 14 drops Angostura bitters

TO ASSEMBLE:

1. In cocktail tin, combine all ingredients except for bitters and dry shake (see page 13).

2. Strain into a double Old Fashioned glass over cracked ice.

3. Top with Angostura bitters and garnish with activated mint top. To activate mint, rub it gently with your fingers or smack against the side of the glass to "activate" the mint flavor and aroma.

✦ **Pepita Orgeat:** In a large saucepan over medium heat, toast 1 cup pumpkin seeds. Add 2 cups water and bring to a boil. Remove from heat and allow to cool. Transfer to a blender, pulsing until seeds are finely chopped. Using a cheesecloth over a large bowl, strain mixture. Measure the liquid and transfer to a small pot. Add in equal amount of sugar as pepita liquid to create a 1:1 simple syrup. When sugar has dissolved, add 1½ oz vodka and 1 tsp orange blossom water. Stir until combined. Cool and store in an airtight container.

HAVING A DRINK WITH...

NEAL BODENHEIMER OF CURE

As a co-founder of Cure, Neal Bodenheimer has been one of the most instrumental figures in bringing the modern craft cocktail movement to New Orleans. His roots—and memories—in the city run deep, and often hearken back to a time when the cocktail scene was a little bit more sports bars and beers than side cars and boulevardiers. Below, Bodenheimer reflects on the antics of his past, while offering predictions for the future.

SB: You're a native New Orleanian. Are there any old bars that aren't around anymore that you remember as being particularly influential in your life?

NB: Nick's [Big Train Bar] is one that comes to mind. It's supposed to be coming back, but it doesn't look like it's going to be quite the same. There are a lot of bars that are still around, but have changed a lot. The Rendon Inn was a big college bar back in the day, and that was my first bar job. It used to be a free for all over there. The family that owned it [at the time] was very tied into the mayor's office, so they just got away with everything. The first time I had a beer in a bar was at The Boot [a legendary Uptown college bar], and I was thirteen years old, which you can't even imagine these days. I snuck over from my parents' house. There were also a ton of pool halls and sports bars over on Jefferson Highway where we would also go. Whenever I drive [that road] now, I just want to open a bar over there so badly. The bar stock—the bones of it all—is so amazing. They just don't make bars like that anymore.

SB: What was the drinking scene like when you finally came of age?

NB: It's definitely changed quite a bit from then until now. There was a time when there was pretty much only one style of bar in New Orleans, especially during that "fern bar" era. Old neighborhood bars kind of adopted that "fern" style where everyone wanted to knock off TGI Friday's. It was dark times as we look at it now when it comesto craft cocktails—I mean, people really wanted some Bailey's in their drink—but it was also a fun time. People had fun.

SB: What does drinking culture look like to you in New Orleans in the next five or ten years? I feel like you have such a long-ranging perspective.

NB: I think the only way to understand New Orleans is that it's a pendulum that swings between preservation and progress. And we've had a really long cycle of progress. It's been great for the bar scene in the city, but I think you're going to see some people long for bits of New Orleans that they had when they were younger. There's going to be a little bit more nostalgia. We've looked elsewhere for a long time, and now it's time to get back to the core.

DRINK AND LISTEN:
Soundtrack to a Night at Cure

New Orleans is a city ripe with music nerds, and a place where a perfectly curated house playlist is a point of pride and (occasionally) obsession. Nowhere is this more apparent than at Cure, where general manager Turk Dietrich keeps a watchful eye—and ear—on the bar's musical selections.

"I always want the music to match the vibe of the room. Different occasions, times of day, and types of crowd can all play into that vibe," says Dietrich. "I think sometimes you have to dictate the mood via the music, and other times you have to play what makes the most sense for the moment. Music can keep people around for an extra round if they are having a good time."

Dietrich outlines below a typical open-to-close soundtrack for a night at Cure, featuring some of the bar's house favorites over the past seven years.

1. "Mother-in-Law," by Ernie K. Doe
During happy hour, we tend to play things like old Stax-style soul and New Orleans soul/funk from the '50s, '60s, and '70s. This classic from Ernie K. Doe always sounds great at the beginning of a shift.

2. "Beeside," by Tintern Abbey
When the sun is shining, psychedelia from the late '60s has worked really well for early-week happy hour.

3. "King in My Empire," by Rhythm & Sound
Over the last few years, dub has become an early evening staple. The minimal, Berlin-style of dub works really well for the atmosphere when the sun is setting.

4. "Eye in the Sky," by Alan Parsons Project

The transition from happy hour to the mid-evening is usually pretty mellow, so playing exciting music can be the wrong move. This AM radio classic is pretty indicative of what I want to hear during that time.

5. "Alberto Balsalm," by Aphex Twin

This is another Cure classic. The chords and the general mood of this track are basically what I wish Cure could emanate 24/7.

6. "Fade to Grey," by Visage

Right before the 10 p.m. rush starts to happen, I like to play things in the realm of sexy, synth pop or Italo disco. When the time is right, I'll play some Chicago house or Detroit electro.

7. "Dance," by ESG

Funk and hip hop tend to work really well as we get into the late-night crowd. This track can set off any party. "Nasty Girl" by Vanity is another great example.

8. "White Horse," by Laid Back

This is one of the funkiest, dirtiest, and sexiest electronic tracks of all time. Sounds good every single time we want people to start moving.

9. "Tuesday," by I Love Makonnen

So many hip hop cuts have become standards over the years. In the last year or so, this has become one that gets the bartenders reinvigorated and ready to make the last push.

10. "Libet's Delay," by The Caretaker

Every bar needs closing music for when it's time to bring the night to an end. This album of digitally manipulated old ballroom music from the 1930s is a go-to for us.

MAGIC TREE

Mastiha, a Greek liqueur made from the aromatic resin of the hyper-rare mastic tree, isn't an ingredient you're likely find on a grocery store shelf. With a noticeable sweetness and notes of clove, however, it is one you'll find yourself returning to time and again after making this cocktail, which balances out the spirit's piney notes with a swish of lime and the cooling embrace of cucumber.

Attributed to Ryan Gannon at Cure.

GLASSWARE: Coupe glass

GARNISH: Bittermens Cucumber Bitters

- **2 slices cucumber**
- **1½ oz Stoupakis Homeric Mastiha**
- **½ oz Suze**
- **½ oz Navy-strength gin, preferably Royal Dock**
- **¾ oz lime juice**
- **¼ oz simple syrup**

TO ASSEMBLE:

1. In the bottom of a cocktail tin, lightly muddle the cucumbers.

2. Add remaining ingredients and short shake (see page 14).

3. Double strain (see page 13) into a coupe.

4. Top with 7 drops of cucumber bitters.

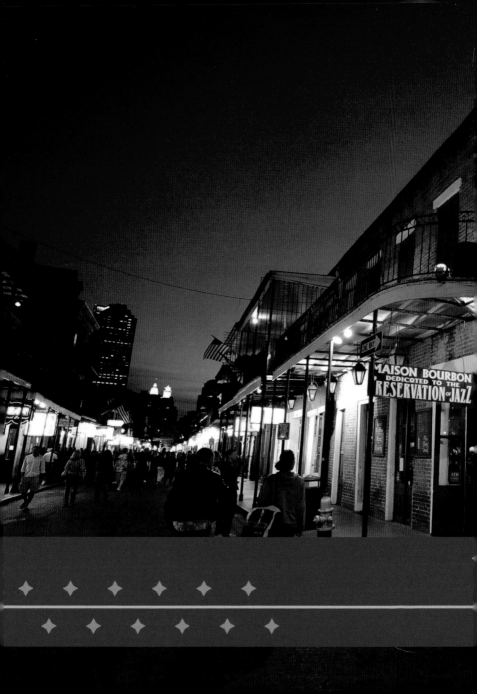

CULT CLASSIC:
ROGUE COCKTAILS

Like a great mixtape or DIY project, *Rogue Cocktails*—a self-published, 2009 chapbook created by Cure's Kirk Epistonal and Maks Pazuniak—brought together some of New Orleans' best bartenders and gave them one instruction: get weird, difficult, and loud with your cocktail creations.

"*Rogue Cocktails* was created at a time that there was a large selection of cocktail books with the same recipes as books 100 years ago. Almost all recipes centered around 'safe' taste profiles," says Kirk. "If we made *Rogue Cocktails* today, I think it would be a little less angry in its manifesto, but what would any punk rock album sound like if made by the same kids ten years later? Maybe more 'mature' but likely less impactful."

The book has gone on to become something of a New Orleans cult classic, capturing the badass, devil-may-care spirit of the city in a way that moves beyond traditional interpretations.

"WE WERE AMBITIOUS AND IMPETUOUS BARTENDERS LOOKING FOR INSPIRATION, AND DECIDED THAT WE COULD BE A VOICE FOR THESE SAID DESIRES."

—*Kirk Epistonal, author of Rogue Cocktails*

THE SCOTCH CRINGE

Yes, naysayers, it's true: in the right hands, scotch can be a summery (and delicious) spirit. The Scotch Cringe proves this in spades, lightening up the spirit's peatiness with the addition of lime and watermelon.

Attributed to Neal Bodenheimer in Rogue Cocktails.

GLASSWARE: Collins glass

GARNISH: None

- **1 whole egg**
- **¾ oz lime juice**
- **2 oz Scotch, preferably Laphroaig 10 Year**
- **¾ oz simple syrup (see page 14)**
- **2 2-inch cubes watermelon**

TO ASSEMBLE:

1. In a cocktail tin, combine egg and lime juice and dry shake (see page 13).

2. Add remaining ingredients and briefly muddle the watermelon.

3. Shake again and strain into a Collins glass filled with ice.

THE VELLOCET

A little bit tiki, a whole lot rock 'n roll, the Vellocet is the kind of well-swizzled, dueling-bitters drink you'll start swearing by for warm afternoons.

Attributed to Kirk Epistonal in Rogue Cocktails.

GLASSWARE: Collins glass

GARNISH: Mint sprig

- **2 oz green chartreuse**
- **1¼ oz pineapple juice**
- **¾ oz lime juice**
- **½ oz falernum**
- **2 dashes Angostura bitters**
- **2 dashes Peychaud's bitters**

TO ASSEMBLE:

1. In a Collins glass filled with crushed ice, combine all ingredients.

2. Swizzle (stir gently) until frost forms on the outside of the glass.

3. Garnish with a mint sprig.

∽ SHADYSIDE FIZZ ∽

Always wanted to work tequila into your brunch hour cocktail rotation without raising eyebrows? Here's your chance.
Attributed to Mike Ryan in Rogue Cocktails.

GLASSWARE: Collins glass

GARNISH: Angostura bitters

- 1 egg white
- ¾ oz lime juice
- 1 oz blanco tequila, preferably Herradura
- 1 oz Angostura bitters
- ¾ oz simple syrup (see page 14
- Sprite, to top

To Assemble:

1. In a cocktail tin, combine egg white and lime and dry shake (see page 13

2. Add tequila, bitters, simple syrup, and ice. Shake.

3. Strain into a Collins glass filled with ice.

4. Top with Sprite, garnish with 3 drops of Angostura.

THE START AND FINISH

The *Rogue Cocktail* fellows like to note this drink is ideal for either starting or ending an evening, making it a rare jack-of-all-hours cocktail.

Attributed to Rhiannon Enil in Rogue Cocktails.

GLASSWARE: Rocks glass

GARNISH: Orange twist

- **1½ oz amaro, preferably Averna**
- **½ oz Lillet Blonde**
- **½ oz dry vermouth**
- **½ oz absinthe**
- **1 dash orange bitters**

TO ASSEMBLE:

1. In a mixing glass, combine all ingredients. Stir.

2. Strain over a rocks glass filled with ice.

3. Garnish with an orange twist.

PARKWAY FLOAT

A spin on the root beer float that's definitely adults only, the cherry on top of the Parkaway Float is the easy-to-make fresh, sweetened cream.

Attributed to Ricky Gomez in Rogue Cocktails.

GLASSWARE: Collins glass

GARNISH: Sweetened cream (see below)

- **2 oz añejo tequila, preferably Tesoro**
- **¾ oz fernet**
- **2 oz root beer**

TO ASSEMBLE:

1. In a Collins glass half-filled with ice, stir tequila and fernet.

2. Add root beer.

3. Top with sweetened cream.

✦ **Sweetened Cream:** In a squeeze bottle, add 2 ounces heavy cream and 1 barspoon sugar. Shake.

THE FALL OF MAN

Unicum is a Hungarian liqueur aged in oak casks and made from a blend of more than 40 herbs. It's simultaneously refreshing and bitter.

Attributed to Maks Pazuniak in Rogue Cocktails.

GLASSWARE: Rocks glass

GARNISH: Expressed orange peel

- **5 swaths orange peel**
- **1 oz bourbon**
- **1 oz Unicum**
- **¼ oz Cointreau**
- **¼ oz cherry heering**
- **¼ oz punt e mes vermouth**

TO ASSEMBLE:

1. In a rocks glass with ice, express oil from orange peels. Then place peels inside glass.

2. In a mixing glass, combine remaining ingredients. Stir.

3. Strain into rocks glass with seasoned ice and orange peels. Stir once.

HOW DOES YOUR GARDEN GROW?
DRINKING NEW ORLEANS' SWEET BOUNTY

Thanks to its latitudinal position, infrequent hard freezes, and bountiful sunshine (dotted with bursts of rain, of course), New Orleans has a growing season that lasts almost year round. While California might lay claim to pioneering the farm-to-glass cocktail movement, it's something that even casual drinkers have been doing for generations in the Crescent City: snipping off mint sprigs to muddle into juleps, snagging a backyard orange to squeeze for weekend mimosas, and picking buckets of finger-staining blackberries for syrups and liqueurs.

The city is bubbling over with natural riches to such a degree that there's even a non-profit, the New Orleans Fruit Tree Project, dedicated to collecting leftover harvests from trees around town so that no good fruit goes to waste.

In this chapter, New Orleans bartenders known for their locally-focused, produce-driven drink concoctions tackle three of South Louisiana's finest offerings: strawberries, satsumas, and local honey.

"IT WAS ONE OF THOSE CALM, BLUE-MISTED, BALMY, NOVEMBER DAYS THAT NEW ORLEANS CAN HAVE WHEN ALL THE REST OF THE COUNTRY IS FUR-WRAPPED."

—*Alice Dunbar Nelson, "Little Miss Sophie," The Goodness of St. Roque, 1899*

STRAWBERRY

CHRISTINE JEANINE NEILSEN, BARTENDER AT ANGELINE (PG. 58)

Strawberries have not one, but two seasons in New Orleans, with the most hotly anticipated occurring from late March through early May each year. During this time, the strawberry epicenter of Ponchatoula, Louisiana, located about an hour outside Orleans Parish, hosts a weekend-long strawberry festival to celebrate the annual harvest, complete with a roster of all-things-berry to eat and drink. (Strawberry wine, anyone?)

It's also the prime place to pick up an under-the-radar local swamp fruit known as the mayhaw, a tiny pink berry which makes a lovely, tart syrup ideal for mixing with gin or adding extra bite to a punch bowl.

⌒ A PROMISE'S GHOST ⌒

The sparkling wine of choice for this cocktail would be Prosecco, but anything bubble-based will do. (There's no such thing as a wrong decision when it comes to sparkling wine.)

GLASSWARE: Champagne flute

GARNISH: Long lemon twist

- **1 oz Pimm's #1**
- **¾ oz pisco, preferably Macchu**
- **¾ oz strawberry Thai basil shrub**
- **¼ oz lemon juice**
- **2 oz sparkling wine, to top**

TO ASSEMBLE:

1. In a cocktail tin, combine all ingredients except sparkling wine. Shake.

2. Double strain into a champagne flute and top with sparkling wine.

3. Garnish with a long lemon twist.

✦ **Strawberry Thai Basil Shrub:** In a large saucepan, combine 2 pounds strawberries, 8 cups granulated sugar, 2 quarts water, and 1 cup packed Thai basil. Bring to a boil over medium-high heat. Cook until mixture is reduced by one fourth. Turn off heat and allow mixture to cool to room temperature, then strain through chinois into a large bowl. Add 2 cups rice wine vinegar and stir until combined. Bottle in an airtight container and refrigerate for up to 2 weeks.

For the less liquor-inclined, this recipe can also be easily crafted into a "mocktail" by combining 1½ ounces of the strawberry Thai basil shrub with ½ ounce of lemon juice and topping with soda.

GLASSWARE: Collins glass

GARNISH: Thai basil sprig, umbrella

- **1 oz strawberry Thai basil shrub**
- **2 oz bourbon, preferably Evan Williams Single Barrel**
- **1 oz lemon juice**
- **Soda water, to top**

TO ASSEMBLE:

1. In a cocktail tin with ice, combine all ingredients except soda water. Shake.

2. Strain into a Collins glass, and top with soda.

3. Garnish with a sprig of Thai basil and an umbrella.

HONEY
KIMBERLY PATTON-BRAGG, BARTENDER AT THREE MUSES

Local honey is invaluable for bartenders in New Orleans, whether whipping up a honey syrup for a toddy, or using it to candy flowers as gorgeous (and edible) drink garnishes. Luckily, you can't go very far without running into a South Louisiana honey producer, with apiaries all along the Northshore of Lake Pontchartrain and sprouting in urban centers as well, from Central City to Broadmoor. I guess we're all so honey-sweet in New Orleans the bees just keep buzzing around our hives.

⮂ FJORDIAN SLIP ⮀

The use of Bjork Birch Liqueur—distilled with birch bark fresh from the forests of Iceland—adds a woodsy, earthy depth to the cocktail's honey-and-rum sweetness, keeping it from tipping over into treacly territory.

GLASSWARE: Coupe glass
GARNISH: Lemon wheel

- **1½ oz rum, preferably Cana Brava**
- **¾ oz Bjork Birch Liqueur**
- **½ oz honey syrup**
- **½ oz lemon juice**

TO ASSEMBLE:

1. In a cocktail tin, combine all ingredients. Shake.

2. Double strain into a coupe.

3. Mount lemon wheel.

✦ **Honey Syrup:** In a small saucepan, combine 1 cup local honey with ½ cup hot water. Stir until thinned and completely combined.

KNIGHT TAKES BISHOP

Tarragon is a criminally underrated herb—especially when it comes to drink making—but plays nicely with both the apricot liqueur and Irish whiskey in Patton-Bragg's creation.

GLASSWARE: Rocks glass

GARNISH: Tarragon sprig

- **2 oz Irish whisky, preferably Tullamore Dew**
- **¾ oz lemon juice**
- **½ oz honey syrup**
- **½ oz apricot liqueur**
- **½ oz sherry, preferably Palo Cortado**
- **1 egg white**

TO ASSEMBLE:

1. In a cocktail tin with ice, combine all ingredients. Shake.

2. Strain into bottom half of tin, dump ice, and dry shake (see page 13).

3. Strain into a rocks glass filled with ice.

4. Garnish with tarragon sprig.

∾ PROVENÇALE GIN FIZZ ∾

A creamy, floral spin on a traditional gin fizz, this cocktail was practically made for al fresco brunch-sipping in a labyrinthine garden (or, you know, a backyard porch).

GLASSWARE: Collins glass
GARNISH: Rosemary sprig, thyme sprig

- **1 egg white**
- **¾ oz lemon juice**
- **¾ oz. honey-lavender syrup**
- **1½ oz gin, preferably Hendrick's**

- **¾ oz. goat milk**
- **¼ oz. cream**
- **2 drops orange flower water**
- **Soda water, to top**

TO ASSEMBLE:

1. In a cocktail tin, dry shake (see page 13) egg white, lemon juice, and honey-lavender syrup.

2. Add gin, goat milk, cream, and orange flower water. Shake again.

3. Double strain (see page 13) into a Collins glass and top gently with soda.

4. Garnish with rosemary and thyme sprigs.

✦ **Honey-Lavender Syrup:** In a small saucepan, steep 1 ounce lavender in 8 ounces hot water. In a small bowl, strain and mix with 8 ounces honey. Store refrigerated in an airtight container for up to 2 weeks.

SATSUMAS

SHANNON MCSWAIN

The size of a tangerine but with a juicy sweetness all their own, satsumas arrive each November in time for the holiday season, decorating trees around town like natural Christmas ornaments. And what a present they are for New Orleanians! People snatch them up by the bagful from roadside stands and supermarkets around town, peeling away the tender flesh and popping them into their mouths as an afternoon snack perfect in the wintertime sun.

These orbs of orange, citrusy brightness are also ideal for drink-making, with a sunset-colored hue richer and more striking than regular orange juice. There's even a Louisiana town named after them. Take that, kumquats.

⌒ NEATO MOSQUITO ⌒

If satsumas are unavailable, tangerine juice works as an adequate substitute that will properly balance out the drink's heavier elements.

GLASSWARE: Rocks glass

GARNISH: None

- **2 barspoons white sugar**
- **1 satsuma (skin on), halved**
- **1 oz vodka, preferably St. George**
- **¾ oz Campari**
- **¾ oz Cynar**

TO ASSEMBLE:

1. In a cocktail tin, add sugar and then place halved satsuma face down. Muddle.

2. Add remaining ingredients. Shake.

3. Double strain into a rocks glass over one large cube of ice.

TUXEDO SITUATION

"**W**hereas the Neato Mosquito is bold, bitter, and a definite slow sipper," says McSwain, "this drink is light, fresh, and effervescent."

GLASSWARE: Champagne flute

GARNISH: Satsuma twist, cilantro leaf

- **8 cilantro leaves**
- **1 oz satsuma juice, strained**
- **1½ oz cachaça, preferably Avua**
- **½ oz simple syrup (see page 14)**
- **Prosecco, to top**

TO ASSEMBLE:

1. In a cocktail tin, combine all ingredients except Prosecco. Shake.

2. Double strain (see page 13) into a champagne flute.

3. Top with Prosecco and garnish with satsuma twist and cilantro leaf.

DRINKING NEW ORLEANS:

PAST AND PRESENT

"Hail New Orleans, [where] for more than a century, has been the home of civilized drinking!" Stanley Cilsby Arthur writes in the aperitif (er, introduction) to his 1937 cannon-classic, Famous New Orleans Drinks and How to Mix 'Em. "The quality of mixed drinks as served in New Orleans has always appealed to sophisticated taste," Arthur writes, "but the drinks and their histories are forever linked with the past of this pleasure-loving city."

Arthur's status as both famed journalist and dedicated drinker means that the work is brimming with equal parts fact, lore, and colorful personal anecdotes as he outlines the rich stories behind the city's classic cocktails and their construction.

I believe Arthur (who was, oddly enough, also head of Louisiana Fish and Wildlife for many years) would be pleased to know that not only do these much-lauded recipes reach into the past, but have been happily jettisoned into the future.

The five old-line cocktails below (of which Arthur makes mention in his work) aren't the ones chatted about on French Quarter walking tours and sought after by visitors from Toronto and Topeka. No, they are the B-sides and black sheep: the drinks that for some reason have yet to find a proper platform for revival among so many gushed-over Crescent City cocktails. In order to breathe new life into the recipes, each has been reimagined by a New Orleans bartender, allowing past and present to co-mingle happily.

"HAIL NEW ORLEANS, [WHICH] FOR MORE THAN A CENTURY, HAS BEEN THE HOME OF CIVILIZED DRINKING!"

—Stanley Cilsby Arthur, Famous New Orleans Drinks and How to Mix 'Em

STATE STREET COCKTAIL

Named after an Uptown New Orleans thoroughfare, the froth from the egg white and ample fruit juice make this drink an acceptable breakfast drink—if you want. "This is the author's favorite warm weather cocktail. He is fond of it in the wintertime, too. In fact, he doesn't know any season when it fails to hit the spot," Arthur (who was not shy about writing in the third-person) says. "Serve in crystal clear glasses. The drink is a pleasure to the eye as to the palate."

GLASSWARE: Rocks glass

GARNISH: None

- **2 barspoons white sugar**
- **1½ oz lemon juice**
- **½ oz lime juice**
- **1½ oz pineapple juice, unsweetened**
- **1½ oz gin**
- **1 egg white**

TO ASSEMBLE:

1. In a cocktail tin, combine sugar, lemon juice, and lime juice. Stir until sugar dissolves.

2. Add remaining ingredients and ice. Shake.

3. Strain into a rocks glass.

∾ NERTZ! ∾

Tangipahoa Parish is best known for their prolific production of oranges and, for decades, a now-antiquated beverage known as orange wine. Stierwalt pulls from the agricultural heritage of the parish in this cachaça-based variation.

Attributed to Scott Stierwalt formerly of Cane & Table.

GLASSWARE: Coupe glass

GARNISH: Expressed orange peel

- **1½ oz cachaça, preferably Avua Amburana**
- **¾ oz pineapple juice**
- **½ oz lemon juice**
- **½ oz grenadine syrup**
- **2 dashes orange bitters, preferably Regan's**
- **1 dash Angostura bitters**

TO ASSEMBLE:

1. In a cocktail tin, combine all ingredients. Shake.

2. Double strain (see page 13) into a chilled coupe.

3. Express an orange peel over glass and mount for garnish.

ST. CLAUDE COCKTAIL

"I wanted to keep a warm weather spirit in my drink, while lowering the proof so that—despite the requisite egg white—it could be a real porch pounder. Adding the liqueur [Suze] gives a refreshing bitterness that will cleanse one's palate on a hot day," says Jonathan Shock.

Attributed to Jonathan Shock at Catahoula.

GLASSWARE: Coupe glass

GARNISH: Angostura bitters

- 1 oz gin
- 1 egg white
- 1 oz manzanilla sherry
- 1 oz lemon juice
- ¾ oz pineapple juice, unsweetened
- ¾ oz lemongrass simple syrup
- ¼ oz Suze

TO ASSEMBLE:

1. In a cocktail tin, combine gin and egg white. Dry shake (see page 13).

2. Add remaining ingredients, shake, and strain into a coupe.

3. Garnish with 3 dashes of Angostura bitters.

✦ **Lemongrass Simple Syrup:** Add 2 slightly-crushed lemongrass stalks to a classic simple syrup (see page 14) mixture.

NEW ORLEANS PRESIDENTE

A simplified play on the Cuban favorite El Presidente cocktail, which calls for the addition of vermouth and orange curaçao, Arthur makes note that the cocktail should be shaken with ice that has been "cracked fine."

❦

GLASSWARE: Cocktail glass
GARNISH: None

- ½ oz grenadine
- 1½ oz rum
- ½ oz orange juice

TO ASSEMBLE:

1. In cocktail shaker half-filled with ice, combine all ingredients. Shake.

2. Strain into a cocktail glass.

"The name came from the politician Lindy Boggs, who was the first woman elected to Congress from Louisiana," says Gillian White. "While she may not have been a 'president' per se, she was a boss, and a very strong Louisiana-born woman."
Attributed to Gillian White at Sylvain.

GLASSWARE: Coupe glass

GARNISH: Orange zest

- 1½ oz white rum, preferably Plantation
- ¾ oz satsuma-infused Dolin Blanc vermouth
- ½ oz lime cordial, preferably Bittermens

- ¼ oz passion fruit syrup, preferably Bittermens
- 2 dashes El Guapo Mojo Cubano Bitters

TO ASSEMBLE:

1. In a mixing glass, combine all ingredients. Stir.

2. Strain into a coupe and garnish with orange zest.

✦ **Satsuma-Infused Dolin Blanc Vermouth:** In an airtight container, combine 8 ounces vermouth with three satsuma peels, pith removed. Store in a cool, dry place and allow to infuse for 4 days, shaking daily. Refrigerate after use.

ST. CHARLES PUNCH

"Years ago this was a famed punch very much in demand at the celebrated St. Charles Hotel bar," Arthur notes. "Don't forget the straw; this drink demands long and deliberate sipping for consummate enjoyment."

❦

GLASSWARE: Collins glass

GARNISH: Lemon wedges

- **1½ oz lemon juice**
- **1 oz cognac**
- **½ oz simple syrup (see page 14)**
- **1 dash orange curaçao**
- **1½ oz port, to top**

TO ASSEMBLE:

1. In a cocktail tin with ice, combine all ingredients except port. Shake.

2. Strain into a Collins glass over ice cubes.

3. Top with port and mount two lemon wedges.

ST. CHARLES PUNCH V. 2.0

The use of orgeat as a sweetener in Yamada's beachy interpretation adds a welcome nuttiness and warmth, making the drink seem almost tropical.

Attributed to Steven Yamada at Ace Hotel.

GLASSWARE: Collins glass

GARNISH: None

- **2 oz cognac**
- **1 oz lemon juice**
- **½ oz orgeat**
- **¼ oz orange curaçao**
- **¼ oz port, to top**

TO ASSEMBLE:

1. In a cocktail tin with ice, combine all ingredients except port. Shake vigorously.

2. Strain into a Collins glass filled with crushed ice.

3. Float port on top.

JEAN LAFITTE COCKTAIL

This drink, named for New Orleans' favorite absinthe-loving pirate, would've surely sated the sailor before a long voyage. "Let us hope that when Jean Lafitte—the bold, bad, Barataria buccaneer—swaggered up and down the narrow banquettes of Rue Royale he had something like [this] in mind," writes Arthur.

GLASSWARE: Coupe glass

GARNISH: None

- **1 barspoon white sugar**
- **2 dashes absinthe**
- **2 dashes curaçao**
- **1½ oz rum**
- **1 egg yolk**

TO ASSEMBLE:

1. In a cocktail tin, combine sugar, absinthe, and curaçao and muddle.

2. Add remaining ingredients. Shake.

3. Strain into a chilled coupe.

Wolf's spin on the Jean Lafitte lightens it up significantly by using egg white while it retains the drink's rum-swigging spirit. *Attributed to Evan Wolf at Company Burger.*

❧

GLASSWARE: Cocktail glass

GARNISH: Peychaud's bitters

- **1 oz rum, preferably Caña Brava 7 Year**
- **1 oz Galliano**
- **¼ oz Herbsaint**
- **¼ oz orange juice**
- **¼ oz lemon juice**
- **¼ oz rich demerara syrup (see page 13)**
- **6 dashes Peychaud's bitters, divided**
- **1 egg white**

TO ASSEMBLE:

1. In a cocktail tin, combine all ingredients and 3 dashes of the Peychaud's. Add ice and shake.

2. Strain out ice and dry shake (see page 13) to further emulsify the egg white, about 5–7 seconds.

3. Pour into a chilled cocktail glass.

4. Garnish with 3 swirled dashes of Peychaud's.

TANGIPAHOA PLANTERS PUNCH

"Aw, Nertz!" A friend of Arthur's from nearby Tangipahoa Parish exclaimed after trying a version of Planters Punch that he felt was inferior. "The dope you wrote [about] ain't a Planters Punch!" A true gentleman, the friend then offered up the recipe for a Tangipahoa-specific version bettered suit to his palate.

GLASSWARE: Collins glass
GARNISH: None

- **3 oz rum**
- **2½ oz pineapple juice**
- **2½ oz lime juice**
- **2½ oz orange juice**
- **⅛ oz grenadine syrup**

TO ASSEMBLE:

1. In a Collins glass filled with crushed ice, combine all ingredients. Stir.

Without a doubt, Tales of the Cocktail—the annual New Orleans-based celebration of all-things-spirits—is one of the most exhilarating conferences you'll ever attend.

There are no snooze-worthy speakers or tedious ice breaker games. Instead, the event (now over 30,000 strong) brings together the cocktail industry's shining star bartenders, drink enthusiasts, and booze-loving scholars to spend a week sharing their passion for the wide-reaching impact of bartending's science and artistry.

In the morning, expect to sip cocktail samples while learning about the history of agave, or how to best utilize herbs in cocktail making. Then, when school's out in the evening, things let loose. Liquor brands couple with bartenders to host events featuring everything from animatronic bulls to giant ice sculptures, with innovation always on the tip of everyone's tongue.

From a New Orleans perspective, Tales of the Cocktail helped to reestablish the city as an epicenter of drinking culture, reigniting the flame for high-quality imbibing and showing off all the Crescent City has to offer to bartenders from across the globe.

In this section, Ann Tuennerman, founder of Tales of the Cocktail, talks about the event's history, its impact on New Orleans, and its wide-reaching influence on the spirits industry.

Q & A WITH...

ANN TUENNERMAN, TALES OF THE COCKTAIL

SB: What was the precursor to Tales of the Cocktail?

AT: It's kind of crazy how it all got started, because it was really an unplanned pregnancy. It initially was a walking tour about New Orleans bars and restaurants. Really, at the time, people knew products like Tabasco, but they had no idea all the great drinks invented here.

SB: What was the transition to the Tales we know today?

AT: That first year, we had a press conference that honored historic bars and rows—mostly ones that had been around over a hundred years. Then, we had two events: a cocktail hour with a lot of drink authors and ten spirited dinners that paired those people with local restaurants. The very first one was in September, and it was hot as all get out. But we got amazing feedback from people, saying, "Oh, you should do this again!" Then it's evolved into what it is today. I think people forget sometimes that we didn't start out with over 300 events. It took patience and 14 years to get to that point. People suggest things, we try them, we don't try them. We say it works, it doesn't work. It's constantly evolving. The structure is basically the same now, but we're always adding and taking away based on the feedback of the participants and what people want to learn.

SB: What are some trends during Tales currently?

AT: We've educated a lot of people, so now some of the things they're interested in are career development, sustainability, and lifestyle balance. Now, people are becoming a bartender for life, not just for a couple years. Things are a little bit more focused on health. The last four years, we've been doing what we call a "health series" and offering yoga and wellness classes complimentary. Things like that, people would have never been interested in ten years ago.

SB: How has Tales impacted New Orleans?

AT: It put us on the map as a cocktail city, and a cocktail destination, which I think people had forgotten. We never abandoned the idea of enjoying a good cocktail. I think it has given a lot of bars, like Cure and French 75, more support. Now a lot more brands come through New Orleans. We have a lot more people moving here because they might have experienced a year or two [at Tales] in New Orleans and learned how to bartend, kind of, our style.

SB: What's one of your favorite Tales stories?

AT: We all love a good love connection, and I get a new story every week almost of, "I met my fiancé at Tales." I mean, we had two proposals in one year [in 2014]! People just meet and connect. This year, I'm actually trying to host a singles party—sponsored by a single malt Scotch—because I still think there's something to the old fashioned meeting in person thing.

SB: I'd come to that.

AT: I think it's just another great example of the connections and the bloodlines that prevail throughout Tales, whether personal or professional.

‿ GUNSHOP FIZZ ‿

"While utilizing bitters as a base spirit is not a new idea, it is something that one rarely sees in contemporary recipes," Kirk Estopinal says of the Gunshop Fizz, which draws inspiration from the classic Angostura Fizz. Just to kick the bitter factor up another notch (because, why not?), the recipe calls for a final flourish of Sanbitter, a fire engine red Italian bitters soda. Ann Tuennerman points to the Gunshop Fizz as one of her favorite cocktails. *Attributed to Kirk Estopinal and Maks Pazuniak at Cure.*

GLASSWARE: Collins glass
GARNISH: Sanbitter, cucumber slice

- **2 oz Peychaud's Bitters**
- **1 oz lemon juice**
- **1 oz simple syrup (see page 14)**
- **2 strawberries, hulled**
- **3 cucumber slices**
- **3 pieces grapefruit peel**
- **3 pieces orange peel**

TO ASSEMBLE:

1. In a cocktail tin, combine all ingredients and muddle well.

2. Set aside for two minutes, allowing the flavors to blend. Add ice, shake, and strain over fresh ice into a Collins glass.

3. Top with Sanbitter and garnish with a cucumber slice.

DAIQUIRI CULTURE: DRIVE-THRU AND SIT-DOWN

Daiquiris—frozen and classic, respectively—are a deeply engrained part of New Orleans culture. Whether visiting a mom-and-pop drive-thru daiquiri shop (where, yes, you can get your frozen, boozy beverage to go), or sipping on a more craft-driven interpretation, the classic combination of rum, lime, and sugar can't be beat to squelch the summer's looming humidity.

In 2016, Tales of the Cocktail launched the New Orleans Daiquiri Festival, a two-day summer event celebrating this cherished cocktail and featuring an expansive selection of high-quality frozen daiquiris in venues around the city. As a preamble to this, in 2015, the daiquiri was the official cocktail tinkered with during the Tales of the Cocktail drink competition, and I was fortunate enough to be a judge. On the next page is a traditional rendering of the drink, and following is the winning cocktail from 2015.

DAIQUIRI

The Daiquiri just might be the perfect summertime three-ingredient sipper. It's worth learning by heart.

GLASSWARE: Coupe glass

GARNISH: Lime peel

- **2 oz rum**
- **1 oz lime juice**
- **½ oz simple syrup (see page 14)**

TO ASSEMBLE:

1. In a cocktail tin with ice, combine all ingredients. Shake.

2. Strain into a chilled coupe and garnish with lime peel.

∽ DESERT LILY ∽

This drink was crowned champion of the 2015 Tales of the Cocktail daiquiri competition.

Created by Spencer Warren.

GLASSWARE: Large plastic cup

GARNISH: Amarena Fabbri cherry

- **2 oz rum, preferably Caña Brava**
- **1 oz aloe vera drink**
- **¾ oz lime juice**
- **¾ oz simple syrup (see page 14)**
- **½ oz prickly pear purée**
- **¼ oz lemon juice**
- **2–3 drops Fee Brothers lavender flower water**

TO ASSEMBLE:

1. In a blender one-quarter-filled with ice, combine all ingredients and pulse until slushy consistency.

2. Pour into a large plastic cup.

3. Garnish with Amarena Fabbri cherry.

CULTURE SPOTLIGHT

MUSEUM OF THE AMERICAN COCKTAIL

If you're looking for a healthy dose of education with your drinking, New Orleans has you covered. Located in Central City, the Museum of the American Cocktail is a part of the larger Southern Food and Beverage Museum, featuring displays on everything from American whiskeys to absinthe. Founded by (among others) cocktail legend Dale DeGroff, the space seeks to, "advance the profession and increase consumer knowledge of mixology while stressing the importance of responsible drinking." It's a must-visit while in town.

BAKING WITH BOOZE:
LIQUOR-FUELED DESSERTS

SALTED PEANUT BUTTER
BOURBON CUPS 194

STRAWBERRY PORT WINE
CHEESECAKE ICE CREAM 197

J ust when you thought New Orleans couldn't get anymore
saturated in cocktail culture—surprise! Recently, a handful of
bartenders have started upgrading their baking activities by
adding booze, ensuring that a person's after-dinner drink and dessert
now can be one in the same.

Sure, we all know the ho-hum classics, from sticky rum cake to
shot-like bourbon balls, but full-time bartender and part-time baker
Meagan Burke of the blog F&B Department whips up the kind of
thoughtful, libation-based sweet treats that are deeply imaginative
without being over-the-top (no molecular gastronomy mezcal foams,
please).

Spend enough time with Meagan's recipes and, pretty soon,
you won't remember a point in life before you knew boozy, sugary
delights like pisco dulce de leche and rum whipped cream were
possible.

"NEW ORLEANS FOOD IS AS DELICIOUS AS
THE LESS CRIMINAL FORMS OF SIN."

—*Mark Twain*

These quick-assemble, brown liquor-infused party snacks are ideal for bringing as dessert to a crawfish boil or picnic along Bayou St. John.

YIELD: 12 bourbon cups

- **1 cup milk chocolate chips, divided**
- **1 cup semisweet chocolate chips, divided**
- **1 Tablespoon shortening, divided**
- **¾ cup peanut butter**
- **2 Tablespoons salted butter, softened**

- **¾ cup confectioner's sugar, sifted**
- **2 Tablespoons bourbon**
- **½ teaspoon vanilla extract**
- **¼ cup graham cracker crumbs**
- **Flaky sea salt, garnish**

TO ASSEMBLE:

1. Line a 12-cup muffin pan with cupcake liners and set aside.

2. Using a double boiler or a bowl placed over a pot of simmering water, melt half of the milk chocolate chips, half of the semisweet chocolate chips, and half of the shortening.

3. Spoon the chocolate evenly among the muffin liners. Lift the muffin pan a few inches off the counter and drop to spread the chocolate out evenly. Repeat 2–3 times. Place the pan in the refrigerator while preparing the peanut butter layer.

4. In a medium bowl using a handheld mixer, beat peanut butter and butter. Add confectioner's sugar, bourbon, vanilla extract, and graham cracker crumbs, beating on a low speed until combined.

5. Remove muffin pan from the refrigerator and press 1½ tablespoons of the peanut butter mixture into each cup.

6. Melt together the remaining chocolate chips and shortening in the double boiler. Spoon the chocolate evenly into each muffin cup. Lift the pan a few inches off the counter and gently drop it back down a few times. Place the pan in the refrigerator for 15 minutes.

7. Remove the pan again and sprinkle each cup with flaky sea salt. Store the cups covered in the refrigerator until you're ready to serve.

8. Allow cups to warm at room temperature about 15 minutes before serving.

STRAWBERRY PORT WINE CHEESECAKE ICE CREAM

Port wine's fortified status makes it a heavy-hitter when it comes to booziness (typically about 20% ABV), but its sweetness ensures that it's not only an ideal after-dinner sipper, but a great dessert ingredient.

YIELD: 1 quart of ice cream

STRAWBERRY PORT WINE SWIRL:

- **½ cup ruby port wine**
- **1 cup strawberries, washed and stemmed**
- **¼ cup white sugar**
- **2 teaspoons lemon juice**
- **1 Tablespoon cornstarch dissolved in 1 tablespoon water**

CHEESECAKE ICE CREAM:

- **8 oz cream cheese**
- **½ cup sour cream**
- **1 cup granulated sugar**
- **1 cup heavy cream**
- **½ cup whole milk**
- **1½ teaspoon vanilla extract**
- **Graham cracker pieces, garnish**

TO ASSEMBLE:

FOR THE STRAWBERRY PORT WINE SWIRL:

1. In a medium saucepan, bring the port to a boil. Reduce to a simmer and stir until reduced by half.

2. In a food processor, purée strawberries while port is reducing.

3. Strain the purée through cheesecloth into a small bowl and discard the solids.

4. Add the strawberry juice, sugar, and lemon juice to the reduced port and stir until combined.

5. Add cornstarch mixture and cook for 2 minutes, stirring frequently, until the syrup thickens.

6. Remove from heat and pour into a clean bowl. Chill the syrup in the refrigerator while preparing the ice cream.

FOR THE ICE CREAM:

1. Combine cream cheese, sour cream, sugar, heavy cream, whole milk, and vanilla in a blender. Pulse until combined.

2. Chill the base for at least two hours in the refrigerator.

3. Churn according to ice cream maker's instructions until desired consistency is reached.

TO ASSEMBLE:

1. Pour half of the ice cream into a freezer-safe container (recommended: loaf pan).

2. Drizzle half of the chilled strawberry port wine syrup on top.

3. Layer remaining ice cream followed by remaining syrup. Using a skewer or knife, gently swirl the syrup into the ice cream.

4. Sprinkle with graham cracker pieces, if desired.

5. Cover and freeze for at least 3 hours.

6. Let the ice cream sit at room temperature for a few minutes before serving.

WHAT TO DRINK DURING CARNIVAL SEASON

Contrary to what the uninitiated might believe, Mardi Gras is far more than a single day of revelry before Lent begins—it's an entire drawn-out season festooned from start to finish in purple, green, and gold, then topped off with a healthy dusting of glitter. Live in New Orleans long enough and you'll likely begin to develop an entire wardrobe devoted solely to proper Mardi Gras costuming, and even the most unlikely candidates (like me) have found themselves the proud owners of wacky things like flowing purple wigs, butterfly wings, and sequin short-shorts. There's no such thing as "too much" during Carnival Season, and the more outlandish something can be, the better.

Seasoned veterans also know, though, that Mardi Gras is a marathon—not a sprint. Beginning on Twelfth Night in January, New Orleanians steel themselves for evening-after-evening of parade watching, bead catching, and—of course—heavy imbibing. In this section are a few cocktails, both new and traditional, that will help carry you through Carnival Season in liquor-soaked style.

"IT IS CARNIVAL IN NEW ORLEANS; A
BRILLIANT TUESDAY IN FEBRUARY, WHEN
THE VERY AIR EFFERVESCES AN OZONE
INTENSELY EXHILIRATING."

—Alice Dunbar Nelson, "A Carnival Jangle,"
Violets and Other Tales, 1895

WHAT TO DRINK ON TWELFTH NIGHT

Twelfth Night marks the beginning of Carnival Season, and is the first day it's acceptable (according to luck and lore) to eat King Cake, the icing-covered official sweet of Mardi Gras. Created by Evan Wolf, this boozy, creamy play on King Cake was an off-menu black market favorite during Mardi Gras 2016 at Company Burger.

KING CAKE MILKSHAKE

King cakes rule Mardi Gras season (and rightfully so), but it's easy to get burnt out trying to properly pair your king cake du jour with the right boozy chaser. This liquored-up milkshake is, perhaps, the best of both creamy worlds.

Attributed to Evan Wolf at Company Burger.

GLASSWARE: Sundae glass

GARNISH: Thick straw, cinnamon swirl

- ½ oz creme de cacao, preferably Tempus Fugit
- ½ oz amaro, preferably Cio Ciaro
- ½ oz Fireball whiskey
- ½ oz Galliano
- 2 dashes Fee Brothers Old Fashioned Bitters
- ½ teaspoon ground cinnamon
- 12 oz vanilla ice cream
- 2 oz whole milk

TO ASSEMBLE:

1. In a cocktail tin, combine all ingredients except milk and ice cream. Place tin in ice bath to avoid dilution and stir to chill, about 30 seconds. Alternatively, combine liquid ingredients ahead of time and refrigerate.

2. In a blender, combine ice cream, milk, and chilled liquor mixture, pulsing until smooth.

3. Pour mixture into a chilled sundae glass. Top with ground cinnamon and swirl with a serving straw.

What to Drink During Krewe du Vieux

A completely NSFW parade known for its naughty jokes, lewd floats, and edgy attitude, Krewe du Vieux is always the first official parade of Carnival Season and the only one that, in theory, is for adult eyes only.

The story of Chris Hannah's flask cocktail, Nighttripper, comes with a side of fanboy and a splash of Santa Claus.

"My flask cocktail for years has been whiskey, amaro, and a little bit of sweet modifier, like Strega or Curaçao," says Hannah. "During Mardi Gras [2010], Dr. John was King of Krewe Du Vieux, and I was really anticipating seeing him. When he floated down Royal Street with the rest of the revelers, I yelled, 'Throw me something, mister!' and he did. I was elated, and instantly 10 years old—

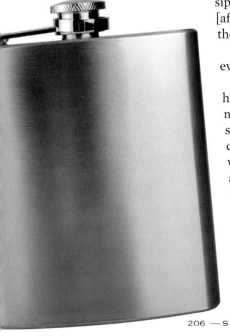

minus pulling out my flask and having a sip. I named my whiskey flask formula [after a Dr. John song] right then and there."

But, somehow, the story gets even weirder.

"When I ran up and yelled to him, he looked at me in a completely mesmerized way. I was so overjoyed with seeing him and catching the throw I didn't care, but was curious about why he looked at me like that. After a couple of minutes passed, I realized it was because I was wearing my Santa Claus costume! It must've been weird for Santa to ask him for something."

NIGHTTRIPPER

The Nighttripper is Chris Hannah's beloved flask concoction. Read more about Chris Hannah on page 34.

GLASSWARE: Brandy snifter (or flask)

GARNISH: Orange peel (or none)

- **1¾ oz bourbon**
- **¾ oz amaro**
- **¼ oz Strega**
- **2 dashes Peychaud's bitters**

TO ASSEMBLE:

1. In a mixing glass, stir all ingredients with ice.

2. Strain over an ice-filled brandy snifter.

3. Garnish with an orange peel.

WHAT TO DRINK ON FAT TUESDAY

One of the most awe-inspiring sights on Mardi Gras
day is waking up extra early to see the bead-and-
feather-adorned Mardi Gras Indians roaming the
streets at sunrise before the majority of revelers make
their way out into the streets. While the costumes
worn by all Indians—from medicine men to spy boys—
are overwhelmingly beautiful, this drink celebrates
the "big chiefs" and one of the city's most precious,
revered traditions.

THE BIG CHIEF

A reference to Mardi Gras Indians, this stirred cocktail is a powerful one and a must-try for anyone with a dark liquor bent. The addition of Averna is a nod to New Orleans' Sicilian heritage. *Attributed to Abigail Gullo at Compére Lapin.*

GLASSWARE: Nick & Nora

GARNISH: Flambeaux orange peel (see below)

- **2 oz bourbon**
- **½ oz amaro, preferably Averna**
- **½ oz punt e mes vermouth**

TO ASSEMBLE:

1. In a mixing glass with ice, stir all ingredients. Strain into a Nick & Nora glass.

2. Garnish with a flambeaux orange peel (see below).

✦ **Flambeaux Orange Peel:** Holding the peel of an orange in your fingers, warm the peel side with a lit match held approximately 2 inches away, over the drink. Squeeze the peel to express the oils over the drink, and drop the peel into the glass.

WHAT TO DRINK DURING KREWE OF MUSES

Ask anyone what Mardi Gras throw they covet more than any other, and the answer will probably be "a shoe." But not just any sweaty sneaker or flip-flopping sandal. What folks are after is a jewel-adorned, glitter-covered brooch handmade by a member of the all-female Krewe of Muses. Displayed proudly in homes and almost downright worshipped, these unlikely treasures are a crafty sight to behold.

Alas, the odds of getting a shoe are slim, but then again, there's always next year. Drink a Rare Stamps to take the edge off.

The unusual star of this cocktail is Cardamaro, a wine-based Italian digestif made from Moscato infused with the quasi-rare cardoon plant (a cousin of the artichoke). Even if you're typically wary of traditional amari, give this nimbler one a go—it's worth buying a whole bottle.

Attributed to the Ace Hotel.

GLASSWARE: Coupe glass

GARNISH: Lemon twist

- 1½ oz Cocchi Americano
- 1 oz rum, preferably Ron del Barilito
- ½ oz Cardamaro

TO ASSEMBLE:

1. In a mixing glass with ice, combine all ingredients. Stir.

2. Strain into a coupe, garnish with a lemon twist.

WHAT TO DRINK DURING DAY PARADES

Day parades are an entirely different beast than those that occur after sun-
down, full of young ones on ladders and in wagons just itching to carry home
piles-upon-piles of loot. This recipe from entrepreneur and dad extraordinaire
Max Messier of New Orleans-based syrup and tincture company Cocktail &
Sons will ensure you have a little something extra to help grease the wheels
when navigating among the toddlers and grabby children hollering for beads
and cups in the noonday sun.

A citrusy drink with a strong hit of lemon, the Streetcar Named Desire is a fine alternative to a mint julep. (I'd like to think Tennessee Williams would approve.)

Attributed to Max Messier at Cocktail & Sons.

❧

GLASSWARE: Rocks glass (or plastic cup)

GARNISH: Mint sprig

- 1½ oz bourbon
- ¾ oz Cocktail & Sons Mint and Lemon Verbena Syrup
- ¾ oz lemon juice
- 4 dashes Angostura bitters

TO ASSEMBLE:

1. In a cocktail tin, combine all ingredients except bitters. Shake hard and fast.

2. Strain over fresh ice into a rocks glass.

3. Garnish with Angostura and mint sprig.

WHAT TO DRINK ON BACCHUS SUNDAY

Bacchus Sunday is one of the most rambunctious of all the days in Carnival Season, thanks to the wine-fueled Krewe of Bacchus' ability to draw thousands out to the neutral ground of St. Charles for music, dancing, and (occasionally) whole-hog roasting on the street car tracks.

Made with madeira, the Sunday Morning Coming Down will set the stage for a day splashed with shades of purple and grapey delight.

Attributed to Isaiah Estell at Cavan.

GLASSWARE: Julep cup

GARNISH: Mint sprig

- **3–4 mint leaves**
- **1½ oz madeira, preferably RWC Charleston Serial**
- **1 oz rhum, preferably Barbancourt 4 year**
- **¼ rich demerara syrup (see page 13)**

TO ASSEMBLE:

1. In the bottom of a julep cup, gently muddle mint leaves.

2. Add remaining ingredients, fill with crushed ice, and stir.

3. Add more ice in a mound on top, and garnish with a mint sprig.

INGREDIENT SPOTLIGHT

OJEN

No one is quite sure just why and how New Orleanians became obsessed with this anise-flavored Spanish liqueur, but it has become an integral Mardi Gras tradition right up there with masks and wacky face paint. This is especially true for members of the Krewe of Rex, who are said to drink it prior to riding each Fat Tuesday. Drink it on Fat Tuesday, but it's delightful any day of the year.

‿ OJEN FRAPPE ‿

An Ojen Frappe is the classic (and simplest) way to enjoy New Orleans' beloved, anise-tinged spirit. Drink it as a toast on Mardi Gras morning, wherever you are.

Adapted by Nick Dietrich at Cane & Table.

❧

GLASSWARE: Double Old Fashioned glass

GARNISH: None

- 2½ oz Ojen
- Barspoon orgeat syrup
- 11–12 dashes Peychaud's bitters, divided

TO ASSEMBLE:

1. In a mixing glass, combine Ojen, orgeat, and 8 dashes of Peychaud's. Stir about 45–50 revolutions.

2. Strain over crushed ice into a double Old Fashioned glass.

3. Top with 3–4 additional dashes of Peychaud's.

⌇ DIRTY WATER ⌇

The passion project of the city's two finest pastry chefs, Lisa White and Kelly Fields, Willa Jean (named for Fields' grandmother) not only serves some of the best sticky buns and ciabatta around, but also has a deep commitment to Southern-with-a-twist cocktails. The duo's commitment to sunlight-hour-appropriate drinks runs so deep, they even operate a boozy slushy machine, which whips up ingenious, Icee-style frozen Rosé—or f'rosé—during springtime.

GLASSWARE: Collins glass

GARNISH: Float of Gingeroo (see note), lemon wedge, straw

- **1½ oz green mint tea**
- **3–4 sprigs fresh mint**
- **1 oz bourbon, preferably Bulleit**
- **½ oz simple syrup (see page 14)**

TO ASSEMBLE:

1. In a cocktail tin, shake all ingredients and pour into a Collins glass half-filled with ice. Do not strain.

2. Top with Gingeroo and garnish with a lemon wedge and straw.

NOTE: Gingeroo is a spice-laden carbonated ginger cocktail created by Old New Orleans Rum. If it's not available in your local grocery store, substitute ginger beer.

MR. FUNK

World-renowned for their robust wine cellar, this cocktail was created in memory of Brennan's late cellar master, Herman Funk. I can only imagine he'd fully appreciate a funk-filled day of imbibing.

❧

GLASSWARE: Rocks glass
GARNISH: Lemon twist

- **1 oz peach vodka**
- **1 oz cranberry juice**
- **Sparkling wine, to top**

TO ASSEMBLE:

1. In a rocks glass with ice, combine peach vodka and cranberry juice. Stir.

2. Top with sparkling wine, garnish with a lemon twist.

"**B**ona Dea was a Roman goddess of fruitfulness and ecstasy whose secret ceremony involved much dancing and wine," writes Alan Walters of Loa. "[It was] a 'ladies only' romp that transpired at the Caesar's wife's house." Deeply herbal and filled with bursts of grassy brightness, the Bona Dea is the drink you should hand-pluck for a romping sing-a-long.

GLASSWARE: Coupe glass

GARNISH: Dill sprig

- **2 oz gin, preferably St. George Terroir**
- **1 oz Absentroux herbal wine**
- **½ oz Suze**
- **½ oz Farigoule Thyme Liqueur**

TO ASSEMBLE:

1. In a cocktail tin, combine all ingredients. Shake.

2. Double strain into a coupe.

3. Garnish with dill sprig.

Boozy BOURBON
STREET ICONS

Yes, Bourbon Street is neon-dripping, inherently over-stimulating, and crawling with people looking to go buck wild, but there are still some Technicolor drinks worth seeking out—if only for a just-this-once, no-place-like-it experience.

"IT IS BETTER TO BE HERE [IN NEW ORLEANS] IN SACKCLOTH AND ASHES THAN TO OWN THE WHOLE STATE OF OHIO."

—Lafcadio Hearn in a letter to a friend, 1879

PAT O'BRIEN'S

718 St Peter St
New Orleans, LA 70116
Phone: (504) 525-4823
www.patobriens.com

The legendary Hurricane at Pat O's is a shade of ruby-pink that almost pulsates, the kind of color a princess-loving little girl would beg her mother to paint her room—then swiftly hate it when she hit 13. For an elevated version, roll to the nearby Empire Bar for Paul Gusting's truly enlightened spin (featuring light rum, dark rum, Peychaud's bitters, apricot brandy, passion fruit juice, honey syrup, and lemon juice) or craft one of the versions below—no waiting in line required.

HURACÁN

El Guapo Bitters is a New Orleans-based bitters-and-syrup company, and this concoction adds a punch of nutty spice to the traditional Hurricane preparation.

Attributed to Scot Mattox at El Guapo Bitters.

GLASSWARE: Hurricane glass

GARNISH: Luxardo cherry, lime wheel, edible orchid

- **2 oz aged rum, preferably Mocambo**
- **1 oz lime cordial, preferably El Guapo**
- **1 oz passion fruit purée**
- **2 dashes El Guapo Tex-Mex Bitters**
- **3 dashes El Guapo Chicory-Pecan Bitters**

TO ASSEMBLE:

1. In a cocktail tin filled with ice, combine all ingredients except chicory-pecan bitters. Shake for approximately 30 seconds.

2. Strain into a Hurricane glass filled with crushed ice, and top with chicory-pecan bitters.

3. Place cherry and orchid on top of drink, and mount lime wheel on rim of glass.

CLASSIC HURRICANE

Okay, sure, go ahead and try the sugared-up, ruby-colored one once. It's fun. But then make yourself a real-deal Hurricane, and taste just how nuanced—and refreshing—the drink can be. I promise you'll never go back.

GLASSWARE: Hurricane glass

GARNISH: Orange wheel

- **2 oz light rum**
- **2 oz dark rum**
- **1 oz lime juice**
- **2 oz passion fruit juice**
- **½ oz simple syrup (see page 14)**
- **½ oz orange juice**
- **½ oz grenadine**

TO ASSEMBLE:

1. In a cocktail tin with ice, combine all ingredients. Shake.

2. Strain into a Hurricane glass one-quarter-filled with ice.

3. Garnish with orange wheel.

BOURBON STREET ICON

TROPICAL ISLE

435 Bourbon St
New Orleans, LA 70130
Phone: (504) 525-1689
www.tropicalisle.com

HAND GRENADE

The Hand Grenade is a hard drink to miss, because every third person on Bourbon Street will be hauling one around. Served up in a tall, orbed-bottomed, yellow glass and advertised by a plush mascot clad like the beverage dancing in and out of the bar, it's quite possibly the most lauded, sugar-drenched, secret-recipe concoction on the strip, and the drink that launched a thousand icy imitations. Be forewarned:
It's easy to down a couple, but the frozen headache the next morning isn't quite so enjoyable.

SHARK ATTACK

Come for the electric blue color, and stay for the plastic shark stuffed down in the glass that can make a fine bath-time play toy after drinking. Just don't be surprised when everyone around you starts yelling out, "Shark attack! Get out of the water!" when you order the drink.

LAFITTE'S BLACKSMITH SHOP

941 Bourbon St
New Orleans, LA 70116
Phone: (504) 593-9761
www.lafittesblacksmithshop.com

PURPLE DRANK

Just about as far down the commercial part of Bourbon Street you can venture, this age-old spot has become better known in recent decades for its wealth of boozy frozen concoctions than its esteemed history as the birthplace of the Obituary Cocktail and ties to the pirate Jean Lafitte. If you're up for it, go all in and get the Purple Drank—a violet, head-spinning trip of brain-freeze delight.

What to Drink During a Sunday Second Line

One of the most beautiful, exhilarating rituals in New Orleans is attending a Sunday second line parade, where gloriously-outfitted members of social clubs dance, drink, and celebrate through the street to the sounds of brass bands.

Second line culture is integral to the fiber of the city, called as much because it traditionally constitutes the group of revelers and merrymakers following behind the "main line," or officially parading band.

On any given Sunday during "second line season" from Central City to the 9th Ward, you can find men in eye-popping lavender suits buck-jumping through the neighborhood next to women twirling feather-covered parasols, past onlookers who have gathered to sip ice-cold beers from coolers and snack on everything from fiery chicken wings to yakamein. If you're lucky, you might even run into my favorite thing: men dancing on horseback! Everyone struts their stuff, and looks mighty fine doing it.

If you want to move beyond nips from a flask, the drinks below will help fortify you on either side of an afternoon spent takin' it to the streets.

BAR SPOTLIGHT

TWELVE MILE LIMIT

500 S Telemachus St
New Orleans, LA 70119
Phone: (504) 488-8114

A true neighborhood joint skirting the edges of Mid-City, Twelve Mile Limit is a low-key spot for finely tuned cocktails that appeals to 20-somethings looking to drink solidly without breaking the bank. Between the pool table, killer jukebox, and outdoor seating area where guests can lounge in giant monster-truck-sized tires, Twelve Mile is a destination for anyone who prefers top-notch drinks with no pretense.

A Sazerac-adjacent, off-menu favorite at Twelve Mile Limit, the ginger liqueur's bite is an unexpected delight.

Attributed to T. Cole Newton at Twelve Mile Limit.

GLASSWARE: Jam jar or rocks glass

GARNISH: Lemon peel

- ⅛ oz **Herbsaint**
- 1¼ oz **rye whiskey**
- ¾ oz **sweet vermouth**
- ½ oz **ginger liqueur**
- 1 dash **Angostura bitters**

TO ASSEMBLE:

1. Coat the inside of a chilled jam jar or rocks glass with Herbsaint, discard excess.

2. In a cocktail tin filled with ice, stir remaining ingredients. Strain into prepared glass.

3. Garnish with a lemon peel.

It doesn't really get more Louisiana than this rum-based, hot sauce-spiked creation dreamed up by Old New Orleans Rum, a local company that's been distilling the sugarcane-sweet juice for more than two decades.

GLASSWARE: Collins glass

GARNISH: Cucumber wheel

- 1½ oz Old New Orleans Spiced Rum
- ½ oz hot sauce shrub
- ½ oz fresh lemon juice
- Soda water, to top

TO ASSEMBLE:

1. In a mixing glass, combine all ingredients except soda water. Stir.

2. Strain into a Collins glass half-filled with ice.

3. Top with soda water, and mount a cucumber wheel on the rim of the glass.

✦ **Hot Sauce Shrub:** In a small, heavy-bottomed saucepan, combine 1 cup hot sauce, preferably Crystal, and 2 cups granulated sugar. Stir over low heat until mixture combines and is reduced by a third. Remove from heat, allow to cool, and bottle in an airtight container.

Jackson Avenue is a thoroughfare that cuts from the Irish Channel through Central City, and is a major artery for not only second lines, but the Zulu Social Aid & Pleasure Club's Mardi Gras morning parade, where coconuts are the highly coveted throw. This cocktail—named in honor of the street—is a drier play on the classic Stinger.

Attributed to Christine Jeanine Nielsen at Angeline.

GLASSWARE: Brandy Snifter

GARNISH: None

- **2 oz fino sherry, preferably Tio Pepe en Rama**
- **¾ oz Grand Marnier**
- **¼ oz crème de menthe, preferably Tempus Fugit**

TO ASSEMBLE:

1. In a mixing glass with ice, combine all ingredients.

2. Gently stir with cocktail stirrer.

3. Strain into a snifter.

THE ZEMURRAY

Named after the longtime king of New Orleans' banana industry, Sam Zemurray, imagine sipping this cocktail under the shade of a banana tree in a neighborhood backyard. Got it? Good. Now make the drink and you're there.

Attributed to Vince Lund, formerly at French 75.

GLASSWARE: Cocktail glass

GARNISH: Luxardo cherry

- **2 oz bourbon**
- **¼ oz banana liqueur**
- **¼ oz Palo Cortado Sherry**

- **2 dashes Peychaud's bitters**
- **1 dash Angostura bitters**

TO ASSEMBLE:

1. In a mixing glass, combine all ingredients. Stir.

2. Strain into a chilled cocktail glass.

3. Garnish with a Luxardo cherry.

SOUNDTRACK: DRINKING AND
DANCING IN THE CRESCENT CITY

Drinking and dancing often go hand-in-hand, and in New Orleans, doing them simultaneously is something of an art form. I can't count the number of times I've seen someone pull off an impressive bump-and-grind or jaw dropping twist to the ground—all without spilling a drop of whatever Technicolor drink they're holding.

First-timers? Just stand back and admire. You'll get there some day, if you're lucky.

"I THINK THAT I MAY SAY THAT AN AMERICAN
HAS NOT SEEN THE UNITED STATES UNTIL
HE HAS SEEN MARDI-GRAS IN NEW ORLEANS."

*— Mark Twain in a letter to Pamela Moffett,
March, 1859*

SOUNDTRACK:

DRINKING AND DANCING IN THE CRESCENT CITY

This booze-infused playlist from Alison Fensterstock—one of the city's preeminent music writers and a veritable font of knowledge about New Orleans sound—traces a wide swath of local jams perfect for pumping at max volume while checking your look in the mirror for a night out on the town.

Getting ready to hit the club? Blasting Big Freedia's bounce classic "Gin in My System" will get you in the proper rump-shaking groove. Looking for a Francophone influence to your tippling? Sweet Crude's "Parlez Nous A Boire" might be calling your name. Is a dive bar more in your future? The jingle-jangling bop of "I Got Loaded" by 1960s doo-wop band Little Bob and the Lollipops will be just the song you need the next morning when you sing along through your hangover, "Last night, I got loaded, on a bottle of gin, and I feel alright!"

1. "LIGHTS OUT," by Jerry Byrne
2. "DEW DROP INN," by Esquerita
3. "I GOT LOADED," by Little Bob and the Lollipops
4. "SHE GOT LOW DOWN," by Huey 'Piano' Smith and the Clowns
5. "COLD BEAR," by The Gaturs
6. "PARLEZ NOUS A BOIRE," by Sweet Crude
7. "GIN IN MY SYSTEM," by Big Freedia
8. "N.O. BLOCK PARTY," by Partners N Crime with DJ Jubilee

THE BAUDIN

With all due respect to part-time New Orleans resident Beyoncé's love of hot sauce, mixing the spicy stuff into your cocktail is some next-level infatuation with Louisiana's favorite condiment. This four-ingredient, sweet-meets-heat sipper is sure to quickly help you get loose.

GLASSWARE: Rocks glass

GARNISH: Lemon peel

- 1½ oz bourbon
- ¾ oz honey syrup (see page 156
- ½ oz lemon juice
- 1 dash hot sauce, preferably Tabasco

TO ASSEMBLE:

1. In a cocktail tin, combine all ingredients. Shake.

2. Strain into a rocks glass filled with ice.

3. Garnish with a lemon peel.

Cheekily named for its oft-maligned key ingredient, Jäger-meister—better known for causing college bros to act a fool than making appearances in craft cocktails—the Great Idea will flip your preconceptions about this spirit on their head. The tartness of lemon and punch of ginger beer proves that Jägermeister can, without a doubt, play well with others—no Jäger Bombs required.

GLASSWARE: Collins glass

GARNISH: Lemon wedge, straw

- 1 oz vodka
- 1 oz Jägermeister
- ½ oz lemon juice
- ½ oz simple syrup (see page 14)
- 2 dashes Angostura bitters
- 2 oz ginger beer

TO ASSEMBLE:

1. In a Collins glass, combine all ingredients. Gently stir.

2. Fill with ice.

3. Garnish with a lemon wedge and straw.

The Pendennis Club is a gin-based cocktail with a peachy hue and plump mouthfeel that derives its name from a hoity-toity "gentlemen only" club in Louisville, Kentucky. For a solid stretch, it was one of the few non-whiskey-based drinks on the menu at Barrel Proof, but don't worry—we fixed that. Behold, the first ever Whiskeydennis, a bourbon-based Pendennis, which has nuttier notes than the original while maintaining the same fruit-forward ethos. *Attributed to Thomas Thompson at Barrel Proof.*

GLASSWARE: Coupe glass

GARNISH: None

- **2 oz bourbon, preferably Old Grandad 100 Proof**
- **½ oz apricot liqueur, preferably Rothman & Winter**
- **½ oz apricot preserves**
- **¼ oz Peychaud's aperitivo**
- **¼ oz lemon juice**
- **¼ oz lime juice**
- **2 dashes Angostura Bitters**

TO ASSEMBLE:

1. In cocktail tin filled with ice, combine all ingredients. Shake.

2. Double strain into a chilled coupe.

WHERE TO DRINK A SET-UP

Like a kind of chilled-out, DIY bottle service, the set-up is a New Orleans institution that makes afternoon imbibing just a little bit more hands-on. Guests order a pint of liquor (say, vodka) and a mixer in the can—from Diet Coke to cranberry juice—and both are served up, no frills, with a plastic bowl of ice and a cup. That's it.

It's then the drinker's job is to play bartender, stirring up their liquor-to-ice-to-mixer ratio just how they please, right there on the bar. If you've ever wanted to experiment with a mixology-driven career change, maybe start with the set-up.

BULLET'S SPORTS BAR
Along with your set-up, you'll find: Tuesday nights this place is crammed with locals and visitors alike dancing to the sounds of the city's best trumpeters, which have included Kermit Ruffins and the late Trumpet Black over the years. **Neighborhood:** Seventh Ward

VERRET'S
Along with your set-up, you'll find: A neighborhood joint that's the historic home of several second line social clubs, it seems like someone is always throwing a birthday party here—and the whole bar is invited. **Neighborhood:** Central City

SANDPIPER LOUNGE
Along with your set-up, you'll find: Home to a family-like atmosphere and some of the city's most stunning neon, Sandpiper harkens back to the heyday of elegant, glowing lights up and down Jefferson Avenue. **Neighborhood:** Central City

WHERE TO LISTEN TO MUSIC, COCKTAIL IN HAND

THREE MUSES
What You'll Hear: The hottest ticket on Frenchman Street for top-notch jazz, it is also is a cocktail lover's dream, with Kimberly Patton Bragg and her team of (mostly) fellow redheads joyously running the floor. **Neighborhood:** Marigny

SIDNEY'S SALOON
What You'll Hear: The new outpost of legendary New Orleans band King James and the Special Men, rock meets blues under the swing of a crystal chandelier. **Neighborhood:** Seventh Ward

BACCHANAL
What You'll Hear: At this stunning wine garden, the young lions of New Orleans jazz play side-by-side with some of the city's funkiest bands all day long. **Neighborhood:** Bywater

HIGH HO LOUNGE
What You'll Hear: Saturday night Hustle dance parties with DJ Soul Sister are the grooviest in town where you can expect to (sweatily) get down to the soulful sounds of Marvin Gaye while *Electric Company* reruns play in the background. **Neighborhood:** Marigny

CANDLELIGHT LOUNGE
What You'll Hear: Ever since being featured on Treme, this place is pretty hopping, but don't worry—it's still a hole-in-the-wall. Come with your dancing shoes on each Wednesday, when the Treme Brass Band plays and barbecue smokes out front. **Neighborhood:** Treme

BENCHWARMERS: UNDERAPPRECIATED
NEW ORLEANS CLASSICS

I f New Orleans cocktails were a basketball team, it's pretty clear which ones would be starters. The Sazerac would get all the pyrotechnics, flames shooting up when it headed out onto the court to an uproar of applause. Cheerleaders would go crazy for the Ramos Gin Fizz. The Vieux Carre would sign autographs after the game.

And then, there are the benchwarmer cocktails. These under-the-radar players are just as much a part of the team but, for whatever reason, have lived in the shadow of their superstar teammates for decades (or centuries).

This year, let's resolve to give these bad boys some playing time.

THE WATER OF THE GULF STRETCHED OUT BEFORE HER,
GLEAMING WITH THE MILLION LIGHTS OF THE SUN.

—*Kate Chopin, The Awakening, 1899,
set in New Orleans*

COCKTAIL A LA LOUISIANE

A sultry, decadent drink that pulls no punches about being spirit-forward, the Cocktail a la Louisiane is what to order once you tire of sipping Vieux Carres.

GLASSWARE: Coupe glass

GARNISH: Brandied cherry

- 1½ oz rye whiskey
- ¼ oz benedictine
- ¾ oz sweet vermouth
- 3 dashes absinthe
- 3 dashes Peychaud's bitters

TO ASSEMBLE:

1. In a mixing glass with ice, combine all ingredients. Stir until chilled.

2. Strain into a chilled coupe.

3. Garnish with a brandied cherry.

ROFFIGNAC

Named in honor of a beloved bon vivant New Orleans mayor, the cocktail (for a brief spell around 1890) sat side-by-side with the Sazerac as one of the city's most notable drinks. A little sour, a little sweet, it's the kind of zingy, berry-bursting concoction that can carry a person through all hours the day.

GLASSWARE: Highball glass

GARNISH: None

- **1½ oz raspberry shrub**
- **2 oz cognac**

- **½ oz simple syrup (see page 14)**
- **Soda, to top**

TO ASSEMBLE:

1. In a cocktail tin filled with ice, combine raspberry shrub, cognac, and simple syrup. Shake.

2. Strain into a highball glass half-filled with ice, and top with soda.

✦ **Raspberry Shrub:** In a medium saucepan, combine 1 lb raspberries, 4 cups granulated sugar, and 1 qt water. Bring to a boil. Cook until mixture is reduced by one quarter. Turn off heat and allow mixture to cool to room temperature, then strain through chinois into a large bowl. Add 1 cup champagne vinegar and stir until combined. Bottle in an airtight container and store in refrigerator for 2 weeks.

⤳ NEW ORLEANS BUCK ⤳

New Orleans is a town thick with a history of rumrunners, where swashbucklers have been sipping (and smuggling) liquored-up sugar cane juice for centuries. This buck is a gingery, nose-tingling tribute to the heritage.

GLASSWARE: Collins glass

GARNISH: Orange twist

- **2 oz light rum**
- **1 oz orange juice**
- **½ oz lime juice**
- **1 dash Angostura bitters**
- **Ginger beer, to top**

TO ASSEMBLE:

1. In a cocktail tin, combine all ingredients except ginger beer. Whip shake (see page 14).

2. Strain into a Collins glass filled with ice.

3. Top with ginger beer and garnish with orange twist.

OLD HICKORY

Named for President Andrew Jackson—who, by report, downed a lot of them when he lived in Louisiana during the Battle of New Orleans—this boozy, stirred creation might be historically overlooked, but will quickly win over vermouth lovers because that's, well, basically all it is. Trade your typical digestif for this during wintertime and thank me later.

GLASSWARE: Old Fashioned glass

GARNISH: Lemon twist

- **1½ oz dry vermouth**
- **1½ oz sweet vermouth**
- **2 dashes Peychaud's bitters**
- **1 dash orange bitters, preferably Regan's**

TO ASSEMBLE:

1. In a rocks glass half-filled with ice, combine all ingredients. Stir until chilled.

2. Garnish with a lemon twist.

 NEW ORLEANS COCKTAILS ELSEWHERE:
DO YOU KNOW WHAT IT MEANS
(TO MISS NEW ORLEANS)?

SHALL BE PRESERVED.

More than most cities, New Orleans welcomes back repeat guests year-after-year, those who, like clockwork, come to spend time with their favorite bartenders, down fresh oysters, and indulge in the flaneur-like charm of lolling away a long Sunday wandering from a crawfish boil Uptown to a downtown Second Line with a fresh drink always in hand.

If you're looking to capture a small piece of New Orleans, these bars across the world allow you to sit, sip, and imagine that you're back watching the boats roll by on the Mississippi.

"NATURE IS THAT WAY IN NEW ORLEANS—

SO IMPATIENT."

—*Grace King, Monsieur Motte, 1888*

NEW YORK

MAISON PREMIERE

298 Bedford Ave
Brooklyn, NY 11211
Phone: (347) 335-0446
www.maisonpremiere.com

"Dreamy" is the first word that rolls off the lips of most people when describing Maison Premiere, a New Orleans-inspired, James Beard-award winning cocktail den and oyster bar in Williamsburg, Brooklyn, that has become a darling of the national craft cocktail scene. Maison oozes a turn-of-the-century vibe, where an elegantly crumbling façade melts together perfectly with crisply polished, black-and-white clad bartenders. It also holds a devotion to absinthe that would make any 19th-century New Orleanian proud, and it is the ideal place in New York to sip an absinthe frappe while splitting a pile of freshly shucked oysters.

MAISON ABSINTHE COLADA

A highlight on a menu filled with tightly-crafted gems, the Absinthe Colada combines the chilly, tropical sweetness of a pina colada with the minty bite of absinthe, helping the drink achieve a depth that Rupert Holmes couldn't have even imagined. *Attributed to Maxwell Britten at Maison Premiere.*

GLASSWARE: Hurricane glass

GARNISH: Mint bouquet

- 1 oz absinthe, preferably Mansinthe
- ½ oz rhum agricole
- 1 teaspoon crème de menthe
- 1 oz pineapple juice
- 1 oz coconut syrup

TO ASSEMBLE:

1. In a cocktail tin, combine all ingredients.

2. Add ice and shake until chilled.

3. Strain over crushed ice into a Hurricane glass.

4. Garnish with a bouquet of mint.

✦ **Coconut Syrup:** In a small saucepan, combine 1 cup coconut cream and ⅓ cup coconut milk over medium heat. Stir until completely smooth, and let cool. Store in an airtight container in the refrigerator for up to 1 week.

~ YELLOW PARROT ~

A Harry Craddock creation that feels equal parts Financial District and French Quarter, the Yellow Parrot is a long-forgotten, three-ingredient Art Deco classic regaining its former, herbaceous glory on menus at appropriately polished bars like Maison Premiere.

Attributed to Harry Craddock at the Savoy, 1930.

GLASSWARE: Rocks glass

GARNISH: Lemon twist

- 1 oz apricot brandy, preferably Apry
- 1 oz yellow chartreuse
- 1 oz absinthe, preferably Vieux Pontarlier

TO ASSEMBLE:

1. In a mixing glass, combine all ingredients. Stir.

2. Strain into a rocks glass over 3 large ice cubes.

3. Garnish with a lemon twist.

~ CARONDELET ~

The Carondelet is named after a New Orleans street that cuts from the Warehouse District through the perfectly-coiffed front yards of the Garden District. Its orange blossom notes add a heady, floral warmth to this decidedly mature drink, spiriting drinkers away on a bike ride past citrus trees in bloom.

Attributed to Maksym Pazuniak at Maison Premiere (formerly, Cure).

GLASSWARE: Coupe glass

GARNISH: None

- ½ oz lemon juice
- ½ oz lime juice
- ¾ oz carondelet syrup
- 2 oz gin, preferably Beefeater

TO ASSEMBLE:

1. In a mixing glass, combine all ingredients. Stir.

2. Double strain into a coupe.

✦ **Carondelet Syrup:** Combine 16 oz orange blossom honey, 16 oz water, 2 heavy pinches Maldon sea salt, ⅛ oz orange flour water, and ⅛ oz vanilla extract in a small saucepan over medium heat and stir until all ingredients combine and slightly thicken. Let cool to room temperature. Use immediately or store in an airtight container for up to 1 week. **YIELD:** 1 quart

NEW YORK

INFIRMARY

1720 2nd Ave
New York, NY 10128
Phone: (917) 388-2512
www.infirmarynyc.com

Yes, this Upper East Side haunt has all of the boudin balls and shrimp po'boys your heart could possibly desire. But it's the fascinating spins on classic New Orleans cocktails that shine, including a breakfast-meets-dessert, bananas foster-themed gin fizz. A host of Sazerac variations riff on the original flavor profile in entirely different ways, from grapefruit and Scotch to Fino Sherry and Creole shrub.

SAN FRANCISCO

BOXING ROOM

399 Grove St
San Francisco, CA 94102
Phone: (415) 430-6590
www.boxingroom.com

New Orleans standards like Vieux Carres and "drive-thru" Daiquiris anchor the menu at this little piece of Louisiana in Hayes Valley, where a daily happy hour serves up specials on drinks (half-priced highballs!) alongside some munchable, Gulf Coast-appropriate fare (think Cajun-boiled peanuts and hush puppies).

OBITUARY COCKTAIL

"**M**ost don't know that the obituary cocktail originated in New Orleans, at the oldest bar in the city, Lafitte's Blacksmith Shop," said Jonny Raglin of Boxing Room. "While its origins might be obscured in folklore, its ingredients make sense. The only thing for sure is you won't find one there now. The boozy slushy machines trump all!"

GLASSWARE: Cocktail glass

GARNISH: Lemon twist

- **2 oz gin**
- **1 oz dry vermouth**
- **1 barspoon absinthe**

TO ASSEMBLE:

1. In a mixing glass with ice, combine all ingredients. Stir.

2. Strain into a chilled cocktail glass.

3. Garnish with a lemon twist.

This easy-to-assemble New Orleans triple threat—rye, root beer, and absinthe—is a highball that packs a three-part punch of sarsaparilla-driven twang.

Attributed to Drew Majoulet at Boxing Room.

❧

GLASSWARE: Collins glass

GARNISH: Lemon wedge

- **1½ oz rye whiskey, preferably George Dickel**

- **4 oz root beer, preferably Abita**
- **3 dashes absinthe**

TO ASSEMBLE:

1. In a Collins glass filled with ice, combine all ingredients. Stir until chilled.

2. Garnish with a lemon wedge.

LONDON

NOLA

68 Rivington Street
Shoreditch, London EC2A 3AY
United Kingdom
www.nola-london.com

This Shoreditch bar is a London treasure, serving up classic New Orleans libations alongside a robust selection of originals, from the Marie Leveaux (rye, dry vermouth, and elderflower liqueur) to the Mardi Gras fizz (genever, fino sherry, maraschino liqueur, lime juice, and champagne), which the menu instructs is, "a fizz to be celebrated all year, not just at Mardi Gras." NOLA also features creations from New Orleans bartenders who have worked guest shifts at the venue, ensuring the (Great) Bayou-to-Great Britain connection remains strong.

LOS ANGELES

SASSAFRAS SALOON

1233 N. Vine Street
Los Angeles, CA 90038
Phone: (323) 467-2800
www.sassafrasshollywood.com

A tavern-style ambiance meets New Orleans tipples at Sassafras Saloon in Hollywood, where a sepia-toned photo of a young girl riding an alligator serves as logo and talisman for the bar. Barrel-aged Vieux Carres and Sazeracs snuggle up against cocktails named with a wink-and-a-nod, including a play on the Paper Plane called the Oaxacan Airboat (Del Maguey Vida Mezcal, Amaro Nonino, Aperol, lime, and agave) and the relatively-sultry Sex on the Bayou (Aylesbury Duck Vodka, Giffard Peche De Vigne, strawberry-lime shrub, cranberry, orange, and lime).

PREUX & PROPER

840 S Spring St
Los Angeles, CA 90014
Phone: (213) 896-0090
www.preuxandproper.com

If New York has experienced an uptick in New Orleans-adoring drinking establishments over the past five years, Los Angeles isn't far behind. At Preux & Proper, co-owner Josh Kopel serves up fare inspired by his upbringing on the bayou, from crawfish remoulade to a po'boy burger topped with—get ready for it—fried oysters. Cocktails include a rye-and-cognac Sazerac positioned alongside a strawberry-infused Hurricane punch bowl. On the next page, Kopel shares his recipe for the Jazz Men, a play on both the jazz musicians so near and dear to the city and the sweet-smelling flower that blooms each spring.

"The inspiration for the drink came from my time growing up in South Louisiana," says Kopel. "There was depth to the experience that I think only a Louisiana native could appreciate. Louisiana is hard to explain and full of layers—some spicy, some sweet—[and] that complexity is represented in this cocktail. It's an homage to my upbringing, really, and a love letter to my home."

Attributed to Josh Kopel at Preux & Proper.

GLASSWARE: Double Old Fashioned glass

GARNISH: Cilantro leaf, pinch of coriander

- ¾ oz lime juice
- 1¼ oz Jazz Man Punch
- 2 oz serrano-infused Ixa Tequila
- Small handful cilantro

TO ASSEMBLE:

1. In cocktail tin with ice, combine all ingredients. Shake.

2. Double strain into a double Old Fashioned glass with one large, square ice cube.

3. Garnish with cilantro leaf laid upright on center of ice cube, add a pinch of coriander on leaf.

✦ **Jazz Man Punch:** In a mixing glass, combine ½ ounce jasmine liqueur, preferably Fruitlab, ½ ounce agave nectar, and ¼ ounce yellow chartreuse. Stir.

WASHINGTON, D.C.

BAYOU BAKERY

901 Pennsylvania Ave SE
Washington, DC 20003
Phone: (202) 664-5307
www.bayoubakerydc.com

1515 N Courthouse Rd
Arlington, VA 22201
Phone: (703) 243-2410
www.bayoubakerydc.com

First things first, Bayou Bakery is a bakery—but one that knows early mornings and fine cocktails go together like cold beer and crawfish. The well-loved sunrise spot slings sweet cornbread, crawfish Monica, and beignets with equal aplomb, pairing them with drinks like the NOLA Swingers (grapefruit, honey, rosemary, jalapeño, and bourbon). They also serve one of the city's best king cakes during Mardi Gras, so get political and get out the vote for it this Carnival Season (or, you know, just eat it).

ACADIANA

901 New York Ave NW
Washington, DC 20001
Phone: (202) 408-8848
www.acadianarestaurant.com

The drinks menu at Acadiana pays homage to Cajun Country as much as New Orleans proper, with a two-step of spice and sass dancing across its pages. Look for the Pamplemousse Rose (gin, grapefruit rose liqueur, and grapefruit juice) and a host of non-alcoholic cocktail options, including the What's Your Passion? (mint-infused lemonade, blood orange, and passion fruit).

RAZZOO

CLUB & PATIO

LIVE CAJUN MUSIC · AUTHENTIC CAJUN FOOD

BALCONY DINING

IQUIRIS PIZZA BEER
OCKTAILS HURRICANES

PIZZA BY THE SLICE

⁓ ACKNOWLEDGMENTS ⁓

The warmest, biggest hug and thank you to Ann Tuennerman, without whom this book wouldn't be possible.

To my always-smiling, adventure-ready photographer, Tammy Mercure, thank you for walking through French Quarter downpours with me to capture all these spots, smiling all the while.

Thanks to The Clash for creating the song, "Train in Vain," which I listened to voraciously while tip-tapping away on this book.

And to the amazing, brilliant bartenders in New Orleans, past and present, thank you for sharing your gifts with us and letting me marvel at your talents on a regular basis. You're what makes this city magical.

INDEX

COCKTAILS

BARS

❧ **ABOUT THE AUTHOR** ☙

Sarah Baird is a writer and editor based in New Orleans. An award-winning former restaurant critic for the city's alt-weekly and seasoned tippling enthusiast, her work appears regularly in print and online for *Lucky Peach, Food52, AFAR, Pacific Standard, Saveur, The Atlantic, Eater, The Village Voice, PUNCH, The Guardian, GOOD, Liquor.com* and beyond. In addition to *New Orleans Cocktails,* Sarah is the author of *Kentucky Sweets: Bourbon Balls, Spoonbread, and Mile High Pie* and *Summer Squash.* Sarah holds a deep, abiding affection for dive bars, and probably knows the perfect drinking song for any occasion.

ABOUT CIDER MILL PRESS BOOK PUBLISHERS

Good ideas ripen with time. From seed to harvest, Cider Mill Press brings fine reading, information, and entertainment together between the covers of its creatively crafted books. Our Cider Mill bears fruit twice a year, publishing a new crop of titles each spring and fall.

CIDER MILL
PRESS

BOOK
PUBLISHERS
KENNEBUNKPORT, MAINE

"Where Good Books Are Ready for Press"

Visit us on the Web at
www.cidermillpress.com

or write to us at
PO Box 454
12 Spring St.
Kennebunkport, Maine 04046